The Mind's Long Journey to the Holy Trinity

The *Ad Monachos* of Evagrius Ponticus

Translated and with an Introduction by
Jeremy Driscoll, O.S.B.

A Liturgical Press Book

THE LITURGICAL PRESS
Collegeville, Minnesota

Cover design by David Manahan, O.S.B.
Christ and Saint Menas, 6th-century Coptic icon, the
Louvre.

This work is based on a larger study Father Driscoll
did of Evagrius' text, *The 'Ad Monachos' of Evagrius
Ponticus, Its Structure and a Select Commentary* (Rome: Studia Anselmiana, 1991).

<u>1</u>   <u>2</u>   <u>3</u>   <u>4</u>   <u>5</u>   <u>6</u>   <u>7</u>   <u>8</u>

Library of Congress Cataloging-in-Publication Data

Evagrius, Ponticus, 345?–399.
    [Ad monachos.   English]
    The mind's long journey to the Holy Trinity :
the Ad monachos of Evagrius Ponticus / translated
and with an introduction [by] Jeremy Driscoll.
        p.   cm.
    Includes bibliographical references and index.
    ISBN 0-8146-2208-9
    1. Monastic and religious life—Early works to
1800.   2. Spiritual life—Christianity—Early works
to 1800.   I. Driscoll, Jeremy, 1951- .   II. Title.
BX2435.E9313   1993
248.8′942—dc20   93-24304
                                                  CIP

Contents

Preface

This little volume is designed as a sort of workbook for a reader who wants to spend the long and prayerful hours which Evagrius' text *Ad Monachos* requires. The core of this workbook is Evagrius' text presented in English translation, a translation which is intended not only to be faithful to the author's meaning but also to provide an English equivalent to the poetic rhythms of the original, thus facilitating a repetitive, vocal meditation and even memorization. But no Evagrian text is of easy access. Thus, I have included here introductory notes which I have tried to keep to a minimum and whose purpose is to move the reader into the Evagrian text as quickly as possible and with a proper and fruitful focus. I would think that a reader may want to read this introduction once or perhaps twice and thus be primed for the adventure of the text itself. After Evagrius' text, there follows a study of its structure, an exercise designed to penetrate the text after the initial encounter. Once into the text there really is no limit to how slowly a reader may want to proceed nor how often the reader may return to the text to explore its many levels of meaning. As the introduction indicates, the proverbs of Evagrius mean to be a father's application of the scriptural word to an inquiring disciple's life. Monks to whom Evagrius offered these words would know that they could return to them with the same kind of profit yielded from continual return to the Scriptures themselves.

You who hold this little collection of proverbs in hand are invited to use it in the same way. Linger with the proverbs. Return to them. Recite them aloud. Memorize some. Recognize more and more the subtle scriptural allusions. Come to know the meaning of the intricate arrangement of their order. In doing this, you will be following a spiritual master toward the knowledge of the Holy Trinity. You will be "an heir of God and a coheir of Christ." (Cf. Rom 8:16-17; *Ad Monachos* 1.)

Jeremy Driscoll, O.S.B.
Mount Angel Abbey and Seminary
St. Benedict, Oregon

Ad Monachos:
An Introduction to
Its Background

General Introduction

Evagrius of Pontus (ca. 345–399) was
educated philosophically and theologically
under Basil the Great and Gregory Nazi-
anzus. He was deacon for Gregory in Constantinople and seems to have been helpful
in carving out the solution to the Trinitarian
problems faced by the council in that city in
381. An amorous attachment to a woman
highly placed in imperial circles caused him
to flee to Jerusalem, where he was received
by the monastic communities of Rufinus and
Melania on the Mount of Olives. Under the
influence of Melania, he retired to the
deserts of Egypt to complete his monastic
conversion; and there he became the disciple
of the two Macarii, living for two years at
Nitria and thereafter at Cells until his death

some fourteen years later. He was among the first of the desert fathers to articulate in writing the wisdom of the spiritual tradition of the monastic movement. His writings, much esteemed in his lifetime and after, eventually came to be the subject of controversy and misunderstanding particularly because of their intentionally enigmatic style. Teachings associated with his name were condemned in the Council of Constantinople in 553.

Ad Monachos is a collection of 137 proverbs by Evagrius, intentionally composed in a biblical style and language, consisting mostly of proverbs of two or four lines, some few being longer. It is a text which introduces the reader into the whole range of Evagrius' teachings. Perhaps at first glance the text does not seem particularly distinguished. The proverbs may strike the reader as being haphazardly joined together, even if occasionally some treating a similar theme may be found to follow in sequence. For a reader unfamiliar with Evagrius' thought and language, some of the proverbs would seem especially bland, others impossibly mysterious. And yet this is a text whose value and interest can only be measured accurately once a key to reading it is discovered and actually used to unlock very rich levels of meaning in each of its proverbs. Then *Ad Monachos* becomes, I think, one of the most interesting texts of the Evagrian corpus; for the reader comes to see that these proverbs are condensations of the already very condensed writings of Evagrius. But not only that. It is likewise seen that the arrangement of proverbs is anything but haphazard. Instead, it represents a very sophisticated presentation of Evagrian themes, together building an image of all the ins and outs of a journey of spiritual progress which begins with the first of the virtues and ends in knowledge of the Holy Trinity.

Ad Monachos is a text designed to provoke meditation, and each of the 137 proverbs is worthy of separate meditation in its own right. Yet the richness of each individual proverb is greatly increased by uncovering the pattern of its placement in the text, which is never without particular purpose. However, the pattern of this arrangement does not appear on the surface of the text. Evagrius means for his reader to discover it. How? By careful meditation, by working with the text, by exercising with the contents of the various proverbs. In designing such a text Evagrius works within a particular tradition, though he himself carries this tradition forward by contributing a new level of sophistication. The tradition of a spiritual father giving a word for meditation is already a large part of the Egyptian desert monastic spirituality to which Evagrius attached himself. But in its written form the tradition is broader. It stands in the line of what the distinguished scholar of ancient philosophy Pierre Hadot calls "spiritual exercises," a key, according to him, for understanding the whole spirit of ancient philosophy. (See his *Exercices spirituels et philosophie antique,* Paris 1987.) It will be useful to focus briefly on these two influences from traditions which have shaped Evagrius' *Ad Monachos:* first, the desert fathers and then ancient philosophy. This is the broad context within which to situate the text. Then there follows a brief summary of major themes in Evagrius' thinking, themes with which the reader must be familiar for a full and proper interpretation of the proverbs. After the text itself in translation, there follows a study of the structure of the whole text, the significance of the order of the proverbs. This structure is the key to understanding the text which Evagrius has created.

The Desert Fathers

The greater part of the writing of Evagrius is cast in the form of apophthegmata: short, incisive sayings from a father to his inquiring disciple. The roots of this form of literature are clearly in oral encounters between master and disciple and in particular in the disciple's request for a word of salvation. The *Apophthegmata Patrum* is probably the best known collection of such sayings; and though the redaction of that text as we know it was prepared in the century after Evagrius' death, it reports sayings from many of his contemporaries and, at least generally, is a reliable indicator of the monastic milieu in which Evagrius lived. Yet it is striking that Evagrius himself is the first of the desert fathers to share sayings of this kind in written form; or, at any rate, his written apophthegmata are the oldest collections that we have.

The interpretation of Scripture is a major responsibility of a father for his disciples. This concern with the meaning and application of particular biblical texts can be discerned in all the strata of the material in the *Apophthegmata Patrum*. Across all the levels of the text—oral and literary—patterns of scriptural events and the language of Scripture are building the framework for the monastic experience. This is true also of the writings of Evagrius and can especially be seen in *Ad Monachos*.

How and where did the monks of the Egyptian desert encounter the Scriptures and incorporate them into their lives? For the monks of the desert, Scripture was not only a written word but also (and especially!) a spoken and lived word. There were certainly copies of the Scriptures in the desert, and many monks had them and made use of them, though certainly not all. But that the text be *lived* as opposed to simply *read* was certainly where the emphasis fell; thus, the famous statement of the monk who sold his copy of the Scriptures and said, "I have sold the book which told me to sell all I have and give to the poor."

The Word of God was appropriated especially through hearing, and this would have happened for monks in three different contexts. First, Scripture would have been heard during the public reading of the Sunday synaxis. Second, there was a daily recitation of psalms and other Scripture which the monk would perform in his cell, usually alone, sometimes with others. Third, the monk would meditate on Scripture, one or two verses at a time, usually reciting it aloud, often while he worked, repeating a verse over and over, digesting it. In these three ways, over many days and weeks and years, the monk slowly became saturated in the language and the spirit of the Scriptures.

In very close relationship with this oral/spoken dimension of the Word of God stand the words of the spiritual father. When a monk requested a word from an elder, the words were received—orally, person to person—as carrying the same weight and authority as the Scriptures. This is because the father's words were seen as being an extension of the Scriptures in virtue of the fact that by the purity of his life the father was a living embodiment of the Scriptures. Indeed, he was a living text.

A father was a father precisely because he was a living text, because by his way of life he expressed the meaning of Scripture. Asking a father for a word was asking him how *the* Word could save the disciple in the concrete circumstances in which he stood, asking how it could save him and change his life. If a father was a father because he embodied the Word, then the word he delivered to a disciple was delivered with the expectation that it too be embodied, that it would be put into concrete practice in the disciple's life. In essence, the disciple was asking for a word from Scripture that fit his life. The master was giving such a word and giving it with the requirement that if this Scripture was to be understood, it must in fact be practiced.

It is to this milieu with its attitude toward Scripture that we ought to look for much of the explanation of the kind of literature which Evagrius has produced in *Ad Monachos*. The proverbs of *Ad Monachos* are certainly polished literary aphorisms, and yet at the same time it is possible still to hear in them their oral roots, that dimension of their being delivered as a living word of Scripture, which was expected to be put into practice. This is the appeal of the text, its power to attract.

The proverbs of *Ad Monachos* are a father's response to a disciple's request for a word. In responding to such a request, Evagrius stayed within the style of desert teaching: he delivered short words which extended the biblical text toward those who received his word. He did this orally as well. But when he needed to respond to a request in writing, he took care—natural writer that he was—to give form and structure to his writing, to take advantage of the possibilities latent in form and structure.

The oral and written dimensions of Evagrius' teaching can be presumed to have worked off each other. With the proverbs of *Ad Monachos* it is not difficult to imagine this process. A monk comes to the cell of Evagrius, shares a problem, and asks for a word. Evagrius, steeped in the Scriptures, offers a word; and the monk departs to practice it. Evagrius returns to what he was doing before the monk arrived, perhaps to chanting a psalm, perhaps to continuing work on proverbs which he is writing. The disciple's problem stays in his mind as well as the word he gave him. A psalm verse gives him a further insight or a key word. He sits down to his writing and refines the word he gave the disciple. He polishes it. It suits the larger work he is writing. He includes it.

This process can be imagined as continuing this way over time. Polished proverbs take their place one by one in the text Evagrius is shaping. Again, a disciple comes to the door of his cell and asks for a word. Evagrius discerns that one of the proverbs he has recently written exactly suits the situation. He offers it. The disciple departs to practice. He has much in the two or four lines he has received. He has words which echo the Scriptures, and he will catch these echoes the more he ponders the proverb. He has metaphors extremely suggestive, metaphors which can lead his thinking down paths more varied than he may at first have expected. He has a rhythm and assonance in the word which make it easy to repeat and remember. He has much to practice.

In short, *Ad Monachos* is a text which must be received as a word from a spiritual master, a word which extends the word of Scripture to the reader. The word's meaning is penetrated only by recognizing the biblical allusions, only by receiving them with the attitude of a disciple, only with a willingness to put the word into practice. (Thus the scriptural index at the end of this volume is a very important tool for meditating on this text.)

Ancient Philosophy

The milieu of fourth-century Egyptian monasticism is the first and most obvious place to look for influences on a monk who wrote in that desert, and yet this is clearly not the only influence on Evagrius. His mind was well formed in the classical philosophical tradition, and there is no doubt that this tradition continued to influence profoundly the theology and spirituality of this monk in a number of different ways. One of these ways is reflected in the sophisticated arrangement and order of the proverbs and the subjects which they treat.

Pierre Hadot's conception of ''spiritual exercises'' as the key to understanding ancient philosophy indicates that a text like Evagrius' *Ad Monachos* needs to be approached with a certain attitude. It is impossible, Hadot argues, to understand ancient philosophy without taking into account the very concrete perspectives, the existential attitude, on which the dogmatic edifice of ancient philosophy is constructed. These perspectives are described by him as philosophy's purpose of exercising those who love wisdom in the practices of learning to live, learning to dialogue, learning to die. Evagrius' text has a similar purpose.

In one part of his study, Hadot deals with the question of the seeming disorder of the various meditations of *The Meditations* of Stoic emperor Marcus Aurelius. He shows that in fact a rigorous law explains all of its contents, for each meditation is an exercise about one or another (or several together) of the three philosophical *topoi* of Stoic philosophy as described by Epictetus. Evagrius' *Ad Monachos* is similarly organized. Key themes of his teaching provide the structure and order of the text. Thus, the various proverbs are exercises on the following themes: (1) the relation between mind, soul, and body; (2) the three parts of the soul; (3) the division of the spiritual life between *praktiké* and knowledge; (4) the eight principal evil thoughts and their order; (5) various levels of knowledge distinguished. The reader who knows Evagrius' teaching on these themes will be in a position to discover the image of the whole spiritual journey which the text creates.

A Summary of Major Themes in Evagrius' Teaching

A number of previous studies have examined and exposed Evagrius' position on these themes. Because he hardly ever expressed himself in a systematic way, these studies have needed to painstakingly gather various cryptic remarks from different of his writings and try to fit them together into some coherent picture. I do not repeat that work here; rather I rely on it. However, for the reader's convenience I briefly summarize here the teachings which must be presupposed for a proper reading of *Ad Monachos,* and elsewhere I provide bibliographical indications for deeper investigations of the material.

Rational Beings: Minds in Souls and Bodies

To understand Evagrius' notion of the condition of human beings and their relationship to God, it is necessary to understand how he uses all the terms listed in the title of this section. For this, it is necessary to know something of his cosmology. A great deal of the material on these issues is found in the *Kephalaia Gnostica* but scattered about. In recent decades scholars have used the more orderly presentation of *The Letter to*

Melania as an interpretive key for the *Kephalaia Gnostica* and for arriving at a general notion of how it fits together. Before summarizing those notions, I would like to offer a remark which can considerably re-orient the attitude with which one reads Evagrius on these questions, particularly regarding the question of his orthodoxy. In general, it is presumed that the Origenist theory of the preexistence of souls within the temporal order is shared by Evagrius. Yet the application of temporal sequence to the relation of mind, soul, and body perhaps risks a serious misunderstanding of Evagrius, who is attempting to speak of metahistorical realities with the language of space and time, i.e., with the only language available to speak of such elusive realities. Evagrius was aware of this difficulty and himself cautions that the mind in its relation to God admits—in the strict sense—the language of neither place nor names. This being said, there are three issues which need to be discussed here: (1) the original creation of the mind, (2) the mind's condition of being in a soul and a body, and (3) a threefold division of the soul.

Original Creation of the Mind. God's first, his original creation, was of reasonable beings (τὰ λογικά). (Here "first" would be not so much a temporal term as a metaphysical and ontological term. For Evagrius, the mind—being the icon of God—must be immaterial like God himself.) These beings were pure minds (νόες) created to know God, to know God as non-numeric Trinity and as essential unity. This knowledge is called essential knowledge. These minds were created equal among themselves in their knowledge of God and in their unity with him.

Mind in Soul and Body. By use of their free will these minds grew lax in their contemplation of essential knowledge, producing a rupture in the original unity and causing the minds to fall away from the essential knowledge and unity. This movement, this misuse of free will, introduces differences in the once equal rational beings. It introduces a disintegration of creation's original oneness and a disintegration of what was originally created as a pure mind. The pure mind disintegrates into a soul which is joined to a body. This situation is described succinctly in a passage from *The Letter to Melania:* "There has been a time when, because of its free will, it [the mind] fell from this former rank and was called a soul. And having sunk down even further, it was called a body. But in time the body, the soul and the mind, because of changes of their wills, will become one entity. Because there will be a time that their wills and their various movements will have passed, the mind will stand again in its first creation,'' (*The Letter to Melania,* 6; trans. by M. Parmentier, 12: 193–198).

As this text suggests, though the disintegration is lamentable, there is something provident in the arrangement, a providence which operates in such a way that body, soul, and mind will become again one entity. These fallen minds were not abandoned by God, who is merciful and provident. In his mercy and through his *logos,* God undertakes to arrange what may be considered a secondary condition for the fallen mind. He provides the rational *soul* as the direct extension of the fallen *mind,* and he arranges lower parts of the soul whereby he joins it (and the mind of which it is an extension) to a *body.*

A soul is joined to a body and established in a world in accordance with the degree of its fall from essential knowledge. This assignment of a body and a world to a fallen mind is called ''the judgment,'' while the whole arrangement, which is designed for the mind's reintegration, is called ''providence.'' In this way there come about the bodies and the worlds of angels, humans, and demons, all of them fallen rational creatures, differing now among themselves according to the degree of their fall and according to the degree of their level of return to their original unity. These bodies are formed of varying proportions of fire, earth, air, and water and by varying predominant proportions of the three parts of the soul. (The three parts of the soul are discussed immediately below.) Thus, angels are formed of a predominance of fire and reason, humans by a predominance of earth and concupiscence, demons by a predominance of air and irascibility (*Kephalaia Gnostica* 1:68). In the proper use of the body and by establishing health in the soul, the disintegrated mind will recover its original unity: ". . . there will be a time when the human body, soul, and mind cease to be separate, with their own names and their plurality, because the body and the soul will be raised to the rank of mind (this can be concluded from the text 'Let them be one in us, as you and I are one') . . ." (*The Letter to Melania*, 5; trans. M. Parmentier, II–12:158–161, citing John 17:22). From our present perspective this reintegration is in the future, i.e., in time; thus, "there will be a time. . . ." Yet in itself, ontologically and metaphysically, it is beyond time (cf. *Kephalaia Gnostica VI:*9).

The Three Parts of the Soul

The platonic threefold division of the soul is a major dimension of Evagrius' anthropology. These are the rational part (λογιστικόν), the irascible part (θυμικόν) and the concupiscible part (ἐπιθυμητικόν). The spiritual struggle of the monk is conceived as a battle for establishing virtue in these various parts. Different virtues are suitably established in a part of the soul to which they correspond, while various vices can also be identified as trouble in one or another part of the soul. The classical expression of this in Evagrius is the *Praktikos* 89, where the various parts of the soul are clearly identified along with the corresponding virtues. This clear statement can function for all other occurences of the terms in the writings of Evagrius.

The rational part is the most noble of the parts of the soul. It is, as I have mentioned, a direct extension of the fallen mind. The other two parts of the soul, together called the passionate part, are the parts whereby the soul is joined to the body (cf. *Praktikos* 38, 49, 78, 84). The mind is extended to a soul in a body as a result of the fall from essential knowledge. By means of a purification of the body and of the passionate part of the soul, the intellectual part (which is a direct extension of the mind) will once again be united to the essential knowledge.

In the proverbs of *Ad Monachos* the terms mind, soul, and body are all used. In each case their precise Evagrian sense is operative. *Soul* is used in no less than twenty-five proverbs. *Body* is used in four proverbs, though the related term *flesh* is found in five others. *Mind* occurs in only three proverbs; but as we shall see, each of these uses is extremely significant. Relying on the foregoing summary, each encounter of these terms by the meditative reader should be occasion for developing a deeper understanding of what Evagrius intends by them.

The Spiritual Life Divided Between Praktiké *and Knowledge*

This understanding and description of the human condition (mind in soul joined to body) is the basis for the various divisions which exist in Evagrius' conception of the spiritual life. There are two major divisions: *praktiké,* where the concern is purifying the passionate part of the soul (thus, *Praktikos* 78: ''*Praktiké* is the spiritual method which purifies the passionate part of the soul''); and *knowledge,* where the rational part of the soul devotes itself to contemplation and knowledge. Thus, the monastic life as conceived by Evagrius is the entire struggle to rid oneself of *evils* (related to the passionate part) and *ignorance* (related to the rational part) and to establish in the soul *virtue* (related to the passionate part) and *knowledge* (related to the rational part). For Evagrius there can be no knowledge in the higher part of the soul without virtue first being established in the passionate part of the soul. So it is that the beginning of the monastic life is concerned with *praktiké,* while knowledge can be hoped for later, after the monk has reached the goals of *praktiké.*

The *Praktikos* is Evagrius' principal work, devoted to this stage of the spiritual life. It can be seen there that *praktiké* basically consists in doing combat with evil thoughts. The first part of the *Praktikos* analyzes eight principal evil thoughts and offers sage advice for how to defeat them. The immediate goal of this purification of the passionate part of the soul is passionlessness, ἀπάθεια. The second half of the *Praktikos* is devoted to a description of the condition of passionlessness. Passionlessness makes true love possible. And only from love can the monk pass on to knowledge. This concern for passing on to knowledge is expressed, among many other ways, by the fact that the

Praktikos is the first of a three part work, the second and third parts being devoted to knowledge, i.e., the *Gnostikos* and the *Kephalaia Gnostica.*

Perfect passionlessness means that health is established in the two passionate parts of the soul: the concupiscible and the irascible. Then these two parts work together to maintain the soul in this state and to leave it free for its higher part—the rational—to function for knowledge. The concupiscible part *desires* virtue and knowledge. The irascible part *fights* the evil thoughts which attack all three parts of the soul. In the passionless soul, thoughts from the passionate part no longer mount up to darken the mind, (cf. *Praktikos* 74) and thereby is the rational part ready to pass into knowledge.

These two major divisions of the spiritual life everywhere obtain in the writings of Evagrius. Keeping them in mind will explain much in *Ad Monachos,* and it is particularly necessary for an accurate analysis of the literary structure, as we shall shortly see. Furthermore, one of the major points which Evagrius wishes to make in the text he has designed here concerns not only the difference between *praktiké* and knowledge but also their intimate connection. We shall see in what follows that among the works of Evagrius none expresses with such insistence the intimate nature of the relation between *praktiké* and knowledge as does *Ad Monachos*.

The Eight Principal Evil Thoughts and Their Order

Praktiké has been said to consist in combatting evil thoughts. *Thoughts* (λογισμοί) is a technical word in the Evagrian vocabulary, its use widespread throughout his writings. It almost always has a pejorative meaning (even if it is unaccompanied by some adjective which secures its pejorative sense) such that the simple mention of "thoughts" in Evagrius generally can be taken to mean "evil thoughts."

Evagrius devotes much space in his writings to the analysis of evil thoughts and to methods for overcoming them. The *Praktikos* is a detailed analysis and set of remedies for each of eight principal thoughts identified by him. *The Treatise on Evil Thoughts* is an equally acute analysis of the way in which demons work through thoughts. So also is *The Eight Spirits of Evil, spirit* being a synonym for *demon* in Evagrian vocabulary. It is a key feature of his theory that to each λογισμός there corresponds a demon or spirit who specializes in it. Thus, to be troubled by a thought is to be troubled by a demon.

The true battle of the monk is with the demons themselves. Thoughts are the means used by the demons to trouble the monk. On the other hand, it is by doing battle with evil thoughts and conquering them (that is to say, battling and conquering the demons) that the monk in fact discovers true virtue in the counterpart of the evil thoughts (see Evagrius' explanation of this in *Praktikos* 82, 83).

Evagrius identifies eight such thoughts: "Eight is the number of principal thoughts in which every thought is contained. The first is gluttony, and after it comes fornication. The third is love of money; the fourth, sadness; the fifth, anger; the sixth, listlessness; the seventh, vainglory; the eighth, pride" (*Praktikos* 6). Evagrius' analysis of these thoughts is keen and filled with practical wisdom, often showing how one thought will work in conjunction with another. There is a certain logic to the order of the thoughts as Evagrius lists them and analyzes them, an order that derives from experience. Thus, for example, fornication follows rather naturally from someone who gratifies his desires for food and comfort. Or if one loves money and is frustrated in his aims to amass it, he will become sad or angry. Vainglory and pride are dangers for the monk who has had some success in his fight against the other thoughts. Thus, in a general way the order of the eight thoughts follows the order of spiritual progress.

Various of the evil thoughts are especially related to one or other part of the passionate part of the soul (i.e., to the concupiscible or the irascible), though Evagrius does not express himself with precision in this regard. Thus, gluttony and fornication can be considered to be in the concupiscible part, as also probably love of money. Sadness and anger are clearly related to the irascible part. On the other hand, listlessness is said to embrace the entire soul, while vainglory and pride are not assigned to any particular part.

The demons have as their goal keeping the monk from reaching passionlessness. So, they attack that part of the soul where the passions reside in such a way as to set them in motion. Evagrius describes this with a language typically precise. *Demons* inspire *thoughts,* and these, when they are allowed to linger, unleash the *passions* in us. The remedy against this system of demonic attacks is a constant vigilance over thoughts, never allowing them to linger. *Praktiké* is learning this art. "Whether all of these [thoughts] trouble the soul or do not trouble it does not depend on us. But whether they linger or do not linger or whether the passions move or are not moved, that depends on us'' (*Praktikos* 6).

Each of the eight thoughts is dealt with in the text of *Ad Monachos*, and they must be recognized as such for a proper interpretation. (The technical terms φιλαργυρία—love of money—and ὀργή—anger—do not occur, but both are major issues in *Ad Monachos*. The same is true of the other evil thoughts. It is not simply a question of mentioning the technical names but of dealing with the issues which these technical names cover.) Also, the order of the thoughts is roughly followed at least in part, in various portions of the text. Knowing this order will help to uncover the structure of the text's entire arrangement. Finally, not only the individual thoughts and their order are mentioned, but the technical term *thoughts* (λογισμοί) is found in no less than nine proverbs. A number of these proverbs play key roles in the overall structure precisely because of the way in which this term is employed in them. The analysis of the structure of the text will make this clear.

Various Levels of Knowledge

When the soul has reached passionlessness, the rational part may turn, unobscured by evil thoughts, to knowledge. Thus does the monk pass from one major division of the spiritual life to another, from *praktiké* to knowledge. Ultimately the knowledge to which the mind is given over is that of the Holy Trinity, i.e., the knowledge for which it was originally created and from which, in its present condition, it has fallen. Yet as the mind returns to this knowledge, it must follow a particular path arranged by the providence of God. The mind in soul joined to body, once having reached passionlessness, must climb by stages through various levels of knowledge until at last it reaches the essential knowledge for which it was originally made.

Thus, there are in Evagrius' understanding two major divisions within the realm of knowledge, the first and highest being knowledge of the Trinity, the second being generally all the lesser forms of knowledge. Various terms cover both these areas of knowledge, and within the lower forms Evagrius distinguishes different levels and different angles of the same level. It will be useful to fix with precision these various terms, for most of them are used in *Ad Monachos*. They are taken here in their upward ascending order, that is, beginning with the point of knowledge at which one enters after having reached passionlessness.

Several general terms cover the whole

area of the knowledge which lies below that of the Trinity. It is called natural contemplation (φυσική) or also contemplation of created things (θεωρία τῶν γεγονότων). (In English the best translation of φυσική seems to be "natural contemplation" as opposed to something like "physics" or "nature." The latter two terms now carry too much of a modern scientific overtone. Contemplation is always implied when Evagrius uses the term φυσική. Unfortunately, there is no single English word which can convey what it implies.) The scope of such contemplation is not the observation or enjoyment of the wonders of nature—though it does not exclude that and even in some ways is based on it—but rather a discovery of the reasons (λόγοι) with which the Logos has made the world. What these reasons show, step by step, is that all things have been made toward the end of leading the mind to knowledge of the Trinity. This contemplation discovers reasons (λόγοι) in bodies and in the worlds and times which they have been assigned. These discovered reasons reveal to the gradually purified and sharpened vision of the contemplative a world beyond the material world perceived by the senses. This incorporeal world, discovered by discovering the λόγοι in the corporeal, reaches far beyond the corporeal world and its wonders.

And this incoporeal world has its own λόγοι waiting to be penetrated. In this knowledge the contemplative sees that in his reality as creature the most fundamental dimension is not his material body. Rather, he sees that in him there is something created, yes; created but immaterial. It is his immaterial mind, and this mind has a reason for being. It is an immaterial instrument made and perfectly adapted for knowledge of *the* Immaterial, God as non-numerical Trinity and perfect unity. The mind is the immaterial icon of the immaterial God.

This movement of the mind upward to a discovery of its own condition as created knower of the Trinity is identified in its various stages by a technical vocabulary. The knowledge which discovers reasons in the material world is called knowledge, contemplation, or reasons of the corporeals. Understanding the reason for the worlds and times in which these bodies are found is called contemplation or reasons of worlds and aeons. The "that" and the "why" of God's assigning fallen minds to bodies of a certain type in a certain world is called the reasons and contemplations of the judgment. Closely joined to this is the contemplative vision that such a judgment is a great act of mercy on the part of God, for the body and its world have been filled, have been provided, with reasons which, once discovered, will lead the mind to the final blessedness for which it was made. Seeing God's mercy and the arrangement of the plan of restoration which it entails is called contemplations or reasons of providence. Discovering the immaterial world and its purposes which lie behind this material world is called knowledge, contemplation, or reasons of the incorporeals, or sometimes also, but less frequently, knowledge of rational beings or seeing intelligible natures. Finally, any knowledge which covers some aspect of the material world is called the second natural contemplation because it treats of a secondary condition of the creation. Knowledge of the immaterial created world is called the first natural contemplation because it treats created reasonable natures in their original condition as knowers of the Trinity.

It is clear that there is a certain logical (λογικός) progress to the knowledges which end in the Trinity. The last two proverbs of *Ad Monachos* state it with a splendid succinctness: "Contemplations of worlds enlarge the heart;/ reasons of providence and judgment lift it up. Knowledge of incoporeals raises the mind/ and presents it before the Holy Trinity" (*Ad Monachos* 135-136). (Henceforth, references to *Ad Monachos* will be abbreviated with the signal M, e.g.,

M 135–136.) This final knowledge is likewise
given several different names. Most com-
monly, of course, it is called knowledge of
the Holy Trinity. But Evagrius also means
Trinity when he speaks more simply of
knowledge of God. He also sometimes speaks
of knowledge of the Unity or the One. The
sense of the word *theology* (θεολογία) is re-
served by Evagrius to refer to the Trinity.
Also, the Trinity is called "the final blessedness."

Clarity about these different levels of
knowledge will help in a number of ways to
interpret with accuracy various dimensions of
Ad Monachos. Virtually all of this terminology
is found in different proverbs of the text. In
order for the meditating mind to follow what
the proverbs suggest, it is necessary to understand what is meant by each of the terms.
Furthermore, the progress from one type of
knowledge to another is the subject both of
individual proverbs and of some of the
chains. These proverbs cannot be interpreted
without reference to these levels, nor can the
chains be identified as chains without aware-
ness of them. Finally, the way in which
Evagrius conceives the whole spiritual life as
a return of the mind to the essential knowledge of the Holy Trinity is a conception
both magnificent and profound in its various
dimensions. This profundity is shared with

the reader. In the structure of *Ad Monachos* Evagrius has created an image of the whole movement of the mind's return, beginning in *praktiké* and moving through many levels of knowledge to culminate in knowledge of the Holy Trinity.

Ad Monachos
in English Translation

**To the Monks in the Cenobium
and in Communities**

1

Heirs of God, listen to the reasons of
   God.
Coheirs of Christ, receive the sayings of
   Christ,
so that you can give them to the hearts
   of your children,
and teach them the words of the wise.

2

A good father trains his sons;
an evil father will ruin them.

3

Faith: the beginning of love.
The end of love: knowledge of God.

4

Fear of the Lord guards the soul.
Good temperance strengthens it.

5

The perseverance of a man gives birth to
     hope;
good hope will glorify him.

6

The one who enslaves his flesh,
  passionless shall he be;
the one who feeds it, by it will he be
  pained.

7

A spirit of sexual impurity is in the
  bodies of the intemperate,
but a spirit of chastity is in the souls of
  the temperate.

8

Anachoresis in love purifies the heart;
anachoresis in hate agitates it.

9

Better the thousandth in love
than one alone with hate in inaccessible
  caves.

10

The one who binds memory of injury to
   his soul
is like to one hiding fire in chaff.

11

Do not give much food to your body
and you will not see bad visions in your
   sleep.
For in the way that a flame enkindles a
   forest
so does hunger burn up shameful
   visions.

12

An irascible man will be terrified;
the gentle man will be without fear.

13

A strong wind chases away clouds;
memory of injury chases the mind from
    knowledge.

14

He who prays for his enemies will be
    forgetful of injuries
he who spares his tongue will not sadden
    his neighbor.

15

If your brother irritates you,
lead him into your house,
and do not hesitate to go into his,
but eat your morsel with him.
For doing this, you will deliver your soul
and there will be no stumbling block for
    you at the hour of prayer.

16

Just as love rejoices in poverty,
so hate is pleased by wealth.

17

The rich man will not acquire knowledge
and the camel will not enter through the
 eye of a needle,
yet none of these things will be
 impossible with the Lord.

18

He who loves money will not see
 knowledge,
and he who amasses it will become dark
 in himself.

19

In the tents of the humble the Lord will
make camp,
but in the houses of the proud, curses
will abound.

20

The one who transgresses God's law
dishonors him,
but he who keeps it glorifies the one who
made him.

21

If you imitate Christ, you will become
blessed.
Your soul will die his death,
and it will not derive evil from its flesh.
Instead, your exodus will be like the
exodus of a star,
and your resurrection will glow like the
sun.

Woe to a lawless man on the day of his
    death.
The unjust man will perish at an evil
    hour.
For as a crow flies away from its nest,
so does the unclean soul from its own
    body.

23

The souls of the just, angels guide;
the souls of the wicked, demons will
    snatch up.

24

Wherever evil enters in, there also
    ignorance;
but the hearts of holy ones will be filled
    with knowledge.

The monk who gives no alms will
    himself be in need,
but the one who feeds the poor will
    inherit treasures.

Better poverty with knowledge
than wealth with ignorance.

An ornament for the head: a crown;
an ornament for the heart: knowledge of
    God.

Procure knowledge and not silver,
and wisdom rather than much wealth.

29

The just will inherit the Lord;
the holy ones will be fed by him.

30

He who is merciful to the poor destroys
    irascibility,
and he who cares for them will be filled
    with good things.

31

In the gentle heart, wisdom will rest;
a throne of passionlessness: a soul
    accomplished in *praktiké*.

32

Craftsmen of evils will receive a bad
    wage,
but to craftsmen of good things, a good
    wage will be given.

33

The one who lays a trap will himself be
    caught,
and he who hides it will be seized by it.

34

Better a gentle worldly man
than an irascible and wrathful monk.

35

Irascibility scatters knowledge;
long-suffering gathers it.

36

Like a strong south wind on the sea,
so is irascibility in the heart of a man.

37

He who prays unceasingly escapes
temptations,
but thoughts agitate the heart of the
careless one.

38

Let not wine gladden you
and let not meat make you merry,
lest you nourish the flesh of your body
and shameful thoughts depart not from
you.

39

Do not say, "Today is a feast and I'm
drinking wine,"
and "tomorrow is Pentecost and I'm
eating meat."
For there is not feast among monks
where a man can fill his stomach.

Pasch of the Lord: passing over from
   evil;
his Pentecost: resurrection of the soul.

Feast of God: forgetfulness of offenses;
he who remembers injury, sorrows will
   grab.

Pentecost of the Lord: resurrection of
   love;
but he who hates his brother will fall a
   mighty fall.

Feast of God: true knowledge;
but he who courts a false knowledge will
   end shamefully.

44

Better a fast with a pure heart
than a feast in impurity of soul.

45

He who completely destroys evil thoughts
   in his heart,
he is like the one who dashes his children
   against the rock.

46

The sleepy monk will fall into evils,
but the vigilant one, like a sparrow shall
   he be.

47

Do not give yourself during a vigil to
   empty stories,
and do not reject spiritual reasons;
for the Lord inspects your soul,
and he will not fail to punish you for
   every evil.

48

Much sleep thickens thought,
while a good vigil hones it fine.

49

Much sleep leads on temptations,
but these the vigilant one will flee.

50

As fire melts wax,
so the good vigil, evil thoughts.

51

Better a man lying down to sleep
than a monk keeping vigil with idle
   thoughts.

52

An angelic dream gladdens the heart;
a demonic dream agitates it.

53

Conversion and humility have set the
   soul up;
compassion and gentleness have made it
   firm.

54

In all things remember your exodus,
and do not forget the eternal judgment,
and there will be no transgression in
   your soul.

55

If the spirit of listlessness mounts you,
do not leave your house;
and do not turn aside in that hour from
profitable wrestling.
For like someone making money shine,
so will your heart be made to glow.

56

The spirit of listlessness drives away tears
and the spirit of sadness shatters prayer.

57

Desiring riches, you will be divided by
care;
and cleaving to them, bitterly shall you
mourn.

58

Do not let a scorpion linger on your
    breast,
nor in your heart an evil thought.

59

Do not fail to kill the offspring of
    serpents,
and you will not go into labor with the
    thoughts of their heart.

60

As fire tests silver and gold,
so temptations, the heart of a monk.

61

Strip down pride from yourself
and put vainglory far away from you.
For the one who does not obtain glory
    will be sad,
and the one who does obtain it will be
    proud.

62

Do not give your heart to pride
and do not say before the face of God,
    "Powerful am I";
lest the Lord abandon your soul
and evil demons bring it low.
For then the enemies will flutter around
    you through the air,
and fearful nights will follow you.

63

Knowledge keeps guard over a monk's
    way of life;
but he who descends from knowledge will
    fall among thieves.

64

From the spiritual rock, a river flows;
a soul accomplished in *praktiké* drinks
    from it.

65

A vessel of election, the pure soul;
but the impure soul will be filled with
    bitterness.

66

Without milk, a child is not nourished,
and apart from passionlessness, a heart
    will not be raised up.

67

In front of love, passionlessness marches;
in front of knowledge, love.

68

To knowledge, wisdom is added;
prudence gives birth to passionlessness.

69

Fear of the Lord begets prudence;
faith in Christ bestows fear of God.

70

A flaming arrow ignites the soul,
but the man of *praktiké* will extinguish it.

71

Clamor and blasphemy, knowledge turns
  aside;
cunning words, wisdom flees.

72

Sweet is honey, its comb a delight;
but sweeter than both is the knowledge
  of God.

73

Listen, O monk, to the words of your
  father,
and do not make his admonitions
  something powerless in you.
Whenever he sends you, take him along;
and travel with him in thinking.
For in this way you will flee bad
  thoughts,
and evil demons will not prevail over
  you.

If he entrusts silver to you, do not throw
   it around;
and if you earn some, give it away.

74

An evil steward will squeeze the souls of
   the brethren,
and the one who remembers injuries will
   not pity them.

75

The one who wastes the goods of the
   monastery wrongs God,
and the one careless of them will not go
   unpunished.

76

The unjust steward distributes badly,
but the just one will give as is fitting.

77

The one who speaks ill of his brother will
  be utterly destroyed;
he who does not care for the sick will not
  see the light.

78

Better a worldly man serving a brother
  in sickness
than an anchorite not pitying his
  neighbor.

79

The foolish monk is careless of the
  instruments of his craft;
the prudent one takes care of them.

80

Do not say, "Today I will stay and
   tomorrow I will go out,"
for not with prudence have you reasoned
   thus.

81

The wandering monk will practice with
   lying sayings;
he will reason falsely with his own father.

82

He who decorates his garments and fills
   his stomach
is shepherding shameful thoughts,
and he does not sit in council with the
   chaste.

83

If you enter a village, do not draw near
    to women
and do not pass time in words with
    them.
For like someone swallowing the hook,
thus will your soul be yanked away.

84

The long-suffering monk will be loved,
but the one who provokes his brothers
    will be hated.

85

A gentle monk, the Lord loves;
but the rash one, he will banish from
    himself.

86

The sluggish monk will murmur much,
and the sleepy type will seek excuses in
headaches.

87

If your brother is sad, console him;
and if he is pained, share the pain.
For doing thus, you will gladden his
heart,
and you will store a great treasure in
heaven.

88

The monk who quits guard over the
words of his father
will blaspheme the grey hairs of the one
who begot him
and will speak ill of the life of his
children.
But him, the Lord will utterly destroy.

89

The one who seeks excuses is cut off
  from the brothers;
he will accuse his own father.

90

Do not lend your ear to words contrary
  to your father's
and do not stimulate the soul of one who
  dishonors him;
lest the Lord be angered by your doings
and rub out your name from the book of
  the living.

91

He who obeys his father loves himself,
but he who speaks contrary to him will
  fall into evils.

92

Blessed is the monk who guards the
   commands of the Lord,
and holy the one who closely keeps the
   words of his fathers.

93

The sluggish monk will be very much
   damaged;
and if he is encouraged, he will even lay
   his habit aside.

94

He who guards his tongue cuts his ways
   rightly,
and he who keeps his heart will be filled
   with knowledge.

95

The double-tongued monk agitates the
 brethren,
but the faithful one brings stillness.

96

He who has relied on his temperance will
 fall,
but he who humbles himself will be
 exalted.

97

Do not give yourself to the trough of the
 stomach,
and do not fill yourself with nightly
 sleep.
For in this way you will become pure,
and the spirit of the Lord will come over
 you.

98

In the one singing psalms, irascibility is
  quiet;
and the long-suffering one, fearless shall
  he be.

99

Out of gentleness, knowledge is born;
out of rashness, ignorance.

100

As water makes a plant grow up,
so humiliation of the irascible raises up
  the heart.

101

The lamp will be extinguished in one
  who tracks down banquets;
his soul shall see darkness.

Weigh your bread on a balance and
    drink your water by measure;
and the spirit of fornication will flee from
    you.

Give wine to old men and carry food to
    the sick,
for they have worn down the flesh of
    their youth.

You shall not trip up your brother
and concerning his fall you shall not
    rejoice;
for the Lord knows your heart,
and he will hand you over on the day of
    death.

The prudent monk shall be passionless,
but the foolish one draws up evils.

The wicked eye, the Lord totally blinds;
but the simple, he will rescue from
   darknesses.

Like a morning star in heaven and a
   palm tree in paradise,
so a pure mind in a gentle soul.

The wise man will investigate the reasons
   of God,
while the unwise man mocks them.

He who hates the knowledge of God and
    rejects his contemplation
is like to one who pierces his own heart
    with a spear.

Better is knowledge of the Trinity than
    knowledge of the incorporeals;
and the contemplation of it beyond
    reasons for all the aeons.

The grey hair of old men: gentleness;
their life: knowledge of truth.

A youth who is gentle bears many
    things;
but a small-souled old man, who will be
    able to stand him?

I have seen the angry old man elevated
    in his time,
but someone younger than he had a
    greater hope than his.

113

The one who scandalizes people in the
    world will not go unpunished,
and the one who irritates them dishonors
    his name.

114

The one agitating the Church of the
    Lord, fire will completely consume
    him.
The one resisting a priest, the earth will
    swallow him up.

115

He who loves honey eats its comb,
and he who gathers it will be filled by
    the Spirit.

Honor the Lord and you will know the
  reasons of the incorporeals;
serve him, and he will unveil before you
  the reasons of the aeons.

Without knowledge, the heart will not be
  placed on high;
and a tree will not flourish without a
  drink.

Flesh of Christ: virtues of *praktiké*;
he who eats it, passionless shall he be.

Blood of Christ: contemplation of created
  things;
he who drinks it, by it becomes wise.

Breast of the Lord: knowledge of God;
he who rests against it, a theologian shall
  he be.

A knower and one accomplished in
  praktiké met each other;
between the two of them there stands the
  Lord.

He who has acquired love has acquired a
  treasure;
he has received grace from the Lord.

Wisdom knows about the dogmas of the
  demons;
prudence tracks down their crafty ways.

124

Do not lay to the side the holy dogmas
which your fathers have laid down.
Do not abandon the faith of your
    baptism,
and do not thrust off the spiritual seal.
Thus can the Lord come into your soul,
and he will cover you on the evil day.

125

The teachings of heretics: angels of
    death.
The one who receives them loses his
    soul.

Now therefore, son, listen to me:
do not approach the doors of lawless men
nor stroll into their traps,
lest you be snared.
Keep your soul aloof from false
    knowledge.
For indeed I have often spoken with
    them;
their dark teachings I have tracked down,
and the venom of asps have I found in them.
There is no prudence and there is no
    wisdom in their teachings.
All who receive them will perish,
and those who love them will be filled
    with evils.
I have seen the fathers of these dogmas,
and in the desert I plunged in with them.
For the enemies of the Lord met up with
    me,
and demons—through their teachings—
    struggled against me,
and I did not see true light in their
    words.

The lying man will fall away from God;
he who deceives his neighbor will fall
  into evils.

Better the paradise of God than a garden
  of herbs
and better the river of the Lord than the
  great river which darkens the earth.

More worthy of faith is heavenly water
than water which Egyptian wise men
  draw up from the earth.

In the same way that someone who
    mounts up round a wheel would end
    up low again,
so those who exalt their words have been
    humbled in them.

The wisdom of the Lord raises up the
    heart;
his prudence purifies it.

The reasons of providence are dark,
and hard for the mind are the
    contemplations of the judgment;
but the man of *praktiké* will know them.

133

He who purifies himself will see
    intelligible natures;
reasons of incorporeals, a gentle monk
    will know.

134

He who says that the Holy Trinity is a
    creature blasphemes God,
and he who rejects his Christ will not
    know him.

135

Contemplations of worlds enlarge the
    heart;
reasons of providence and judgment lift
    it up.

136

Knowledge of incorporeals raises the
mind
and presents it before the Holy Trinity.

137

Remember the one who has given you in
the Lord clear proverbs,
and do not forget my lowly soul in the
hour of prayer.

The Structure of the Text:
A Key to Its Meaning

What follows now are indications of some of the major structural elements of the text, designed as an exercise to deepen one's knowledge of the text's purpose and possible uses. In following these indications the reader will be best served by a willingness to make frequent reference to the text of *Ad Monachos*. In this way an understanding of the significance of the structure is gradually acquired, and then each of the 137 proverbs can be meditated upon within a wider range of interpretation and with consequent greater profit.

Overview

It is useful first of all to be aware of the overall structure of the entire text. The first two proverbs, M 1-2, echo in their lan-

guage the opening of the biblical book of
Proverbs and can be considered as introduc-
tions to the whole text (cf. Prov 1:1-2, 5-6).
They place in parallel "the reasons (or
words) of God" with "the sayings of Christ"
and these in turn with "the words of the
wise," i.e., with the words of the fathers: the
proverbs which follow. The last saying,
M 137, is a conclusion to the whole and specifically identifies the genre as proverbs.
Within these opening and concluding
proverbs the rest of the spiritual exercise is
arranged in two large blocks. These blocks
concentrate on separate but related themes
both of which are embraced in the two lines
of M 3, the first proverb of the text after the
introductory ones. M 3 reads, "Faith: the
beginning of love./ The end of love: knowledge of God." "Faith: the beginning of
love" is basically the theme of the meditations in the first major block of the text,
which extends from M 3 to M 106. "The
end of love: knowledge of God" is the basic
theme of the meditations in the second
block, which extends from M 107 to M 136.

The reader for whom Evagrius would
have prepared this collection would recognize
in M 3 terms which are linchpins in
Evagrius' understanding of the journey of
the mind's return to God. *Faith* is the first of
the virtues. *Love* is the goal of the life of

praktiké. *Knowledge of God* is the monk's ultimate goal. In other words, the two major blocks of the text are exercises on the two major divisions of the spiritual life as conceived by Evagrius. But neither in *Ad Monachos* nor in any of the writings of Evagrius is it simply a question of first one and then the other. The meditations of the first block again and again suggest the goal which lies beyond *praktiké*; namely, knowledge. And the meditations of the second block remind the monk that he can neither remain in knowledge or progress in it unless he continues to fulfill the requirements of love.

The flow of proverbs in these two blocks is examined now with attention drawn to some of the more interesting features.

First Block, Section 1: M 3 to M 72

Within the first block two distinguishable sections emerge in the meditation. It will be convenient to treat the material of these sections separately and under several different headings.

Chains Interlacing Love and Temperance as Virtues in the Passionate Part of the Soul (M 3 to M 53). M 3 not only embraces the whole movement of the text, but it is likewise the first proverb in a movement which is developed in the proverbs which immediately follow. It was mentioned that faith is the first of the virtues, but Evagrius understands that many virtues stand along the way between it and the monk's attaining love. These virtues are mentioned in the prologue to the *Praktikos* in an order which Evagrius consistently maintains. He says, "Fear of God (ὁ φόβος ὁ τοῦ Θεοῦ), children, strengthens faith (πίστις); and temperance (ἐγκράτεια) in turn strengthens this fear; and perseverance (ὑπομονή) and hope (ἐλπίς) make this unswerving; and from these passionlessness (ἀπάθεια) is born; and passionlessness has love (ἀγάπη) as its child. . ." (*Praktikos*, Prologue, n. 8). M 4 to M 6 are meditations on this chain of virtues in this same order, bringing the meditator to passionlessness. M 7 swings the meditator back to temperance, and M 8 and 9 deal directly with the goal of this chain of virtues; namely, love.

The proverbs move back and forth for some time now among various angles of these virtues, exercising now one aspect, now another. (The movement can be considered as extending at least until M 54 where a different plan of arrangement comes more to the fore.) There are a number of different chains intertwined together here, but we stay close to the thinking of Evagrius in recognizing them as primarily concerned with establishing virtue in the two parts of what he calls the passionate part of the soul. Evagrius speaks of the soul sometimes in a twofold division, sometimes in a threefold division. If twofold, the parts are the rational and the passionate. If threefold, it is because he works with a subdivision in the passionate part; namely, the irascible and the concupiscible (cf. *Praktikos* 35–38, 89). The principle virtue of the irascible part is love; the principle virtue of the concupiscible part is temperance. "It is by the senses that the passions are naturally set in motion. And if love and temperance are present, the passions will not move; but if they are absent, then the passions move" (*Praktikos* 38).

It is not only with the words *love* and *temperance* that such themes are interwoven. Rather more it is the case that a number of concerns of the virtuous life are located in one or another part of the soul whose principle virtues are love and temperance. Thus, for example, *Ad Monachos* especially stresses gentleness (πραΰτης) as a practical expression of love. The theme is placed evenly throughout the text (see M 12, 31, 34, 53, 85, 99, 107, 111, 112, 133). Or other proverbs speak about actual amounts of sleep or food and drink which the monk ought to take. What is especially interesting about this part of the exercise is the way in which Evagrius overlaps the themes and intertwines them one with another. *Ad Monachos* is an exercise which refuses to let the monk focus his attention only on temperance. On the other hand, it never lets him forget its importance. Let us observe some examples of how chains of these various themes are combined.

M 8 is a proverb contrasting love and hate: "Withdrawal (ἀναχώρησις) in love purifies the heart; withdrawal with hate agitates it." M 9 is similarly constructed around love contrasted with hate, and then M 10 mentions a specific manifestation of hate: memory of injury. M 11—"Do not give much food to your body"—will seem a haphazard intrusion into this development unless it is recognized that its concern is with the concupiscible, the other dimension of the passionate part of the soul. The next proverb brings the meditating mind back to the irascible part, using the term itself, lest there be any doubt: "An irascible man will be terrified;/ the gentle man will be without fear." The opposing terms *gentle* and *irascible* of this proverb—like love contrasted with hate— unfold in M 13 to M 15, which are proverbs developing the concreteness of the aforementioned "memory of injury" (M 10). In a system where the ultimate goal is knowledge, very strong indeed is M 13's statement,

"Memory of injury chases the mind from knowledge." M 14 moves on to suggest a plan for being forgetful of injuries, while M 15 presents an actual plan for achieving reconciliation.

The next three proverbs form a chain by contrasting poverty and wealth, and thus introduce a new dimension of the themes. Yet the first proverb of the chain, M 16, is phrased in such a way that it is not difficult also to recognize the link with what has preceded: "Just as love rejoices in poverty,/ so hate is pleased by wealth." The next two proverbs establish a direct link to knowledge: "The rich man will not acquire knowledge" (M 17); "He who loves money will not see knowledge" (M 18). The issue of poverty vs. wealth seems to be a theme which touches both the concupiscible and the irascible parts of the soul. This is made clear for the careful reader in two ways. The formulation of M 18—"He who loves money" (Ὁ φιλῶν ἀργύριον)—means to echo one of the eight principle thoughts or demons which Evagrius identifies—ἡ φιλαργυρία, love of money—a problem located in the concupiscible part of the soul (*Praktikos* 9). But shortly after, an even lengthier chain is formed around the issue of poverty vs. wealth. This is M 25 to M 30. Its first and last members indicate that at issue is also the concrete expression of love, here seen in concern for the poor. And love is virtue in the irascible part of the soul. M 25 reads, "The monk who gives no alms will himself be in need,/ but the one who feeds the poor will inherit treasures." M 30, the last link of the chain, reads, "He who is merciful to the poor destroys irascibility."

The process of unfolding continues with a very strong proverb, M 31: "In the gentle heart, wisdom will rest;/ a throne of passionlessness: a soul accomplished in *praktiké* (ψυχὴ πρακτική)." There is the strong verbal link between *irascibility* in the previous proverb and *gentleness* in this one. Yet even more is happening: M 31 is a sort of summary of all that has gone before in the text. Irascibility, gentleness, wealth, poverty, knowledge, memory of injury, forgetfulness of injury, love, hate, wisdom, passionlessness—all these notions are swirling around together now in the mind of the careful meditator. Hearing the one word can evoke the other. The different words in proverbs side by side help the connection of the various concepts to sink deeply into the mind.

M 31 acts as a summary of all this by bringing together in one proverb key words whose importance has already been highlighted. *Gentleness* is combined with *wisdom,* a word whose striking appearance in the first proverb set a tone for the whole collection.

Passionlessness, which is the proximate goal of the life of *praktiké,* appears again. And for the first time in the text the important Evagrian word *praktiké* (πρακτική) occurs, the technical term which sums up the whole first phase of the monastic life. The next proverbs continue to exercise the contrast between the irascible and the gentle: "Better a gentle worldly man/ than an irascible and wrathful monk" (M 34). The proverb following shows that what is ultimately at stake is knowledge itself: "Irascibility scatters knowledge;/ long-suffering gathers it" (M 35). (Long-suffering is consistently associated with gentleness throughout Evagrius' writings. In *Ad Monachos* compare M 34 to M 36 with M 98 to M 100. *Long-suffering* is the traditional English translation of the Greek μακροθυμία, implying an enlarged irascible part.)

The next chain extends from M 38 to M 44. This is a beautiful and subtle chain which begins with very concrete remarks about wine and meat but which climbs quickly under the metaphor of a feast to several especially striking proverbs about love and knowledge. M 38 and 39 begin the development with the concerns of temperance: "Let not wine gladden you/ and let not meat make you merry" (M 38). "Do not say, 'Today is a feast and I'm drinking wine,/ and tomorrow is Pentecost and I'm eating meat.'/ For there is no feast among monks/ where a man can fill his stomach" (M 39). This proverb introduces the theme of feasting which will figure in the remaining proverbs of the chain. A feast cannot be an excuse for monks to take wine and meat. For monks *feast* cannot have a material meaning, something like filling one's stomach. The following proverbs define what a real feast is. It is described in terms of Pasch and Pentecost. "The Pasch of the Lord is the passing over from evil;/ his Pentecost, the resurrection of the soul" (M 40). This becomes more concrete in the next proverb in terms which have already been heard. "Feast of God: forgetfulness of offenses" (M 41). The next proverb contrasts love and hate again: "Pentecost of the Lord: resurrection of love;/ but he who hates his brother will fall a mighty fall" (M 42). And all this builds to what is always the ultimate goal in the Evagrian scheme: "Feast of God: true knowledge" (M 43). So, the chain which began using an image suited to *temperance* (feasts) has become a chain about *love* and how this leads to *knowledge*. By this point in the spiritual exercise, virtues in the two dimensions of the passionate part of the soul could hardly be more tightly intertwined.

Proverbs Following the Order of the Evil Thoughts
(*M* 54 *to M* 62). In his work the *Praktikos,*
Evagrius gives his classical treatment of the
eight principal evil thoughts (λογισμοί) or demons which trouble the monk. The order in
which these thoughts afflict the monk has a
certain logic to it, and in so saying Evagrius
is clearly speaking from experience and close
observation. The arrangement of proverbs in
Ad Monachos does not follow this order exactly, and yet at a certain point in the text
the last three evil thoughts are the subject of
a series of proverbs. These are listlessness
(ἀκηδία), vainglory (κενοδοξία), and pride
(ὑπερηφανία); and because listlessness and
vainglory have a special relation to another
of the thoughts, sadness (λύπη), it too is intertwined in the meditations. The proverbs
in question extend from M 54 to M 62.

The intertwining of the themes is intricate and deserving of careful analysis, but
here at least the progress of the movement
can be observed. M 54 to M 56 are proverbs
forming a chain on listlessness. The last
member of this chain mentions also sadness,
a theme developed in the next, M 57. M 58
to M 60 are proverbs directed against evil
thoughts in general. Such a chain is well
placed here since for Evagrius there is a sort
of dividing line between the types of
thoughts which precede listlessness and those

which follow (cf. *Praktikos* 12–14). Those which follow are vainglory and pride, and what the monk can become vain and proud about is that he has conquered the preceding thoughts. So, this general chain about evil thoughts signals the divide before the meditation turns to two proverbs concerned with vainglory and pride, M 61 and 62. M 62 is a powerfully constructed proverb and effectively placed. It is the last proverb to precede an extended and intricately developed chain, M 63 to M 72, which stands at the center of the whole collection and speaks so eloquently of the relation between *praktiké* and knowledge. Pride will always be a temptation for a monk who has entered into knowledge. If he gives way to it, "the Lord will abandon his soul behind and evil demons will bring it low." With this severe warning and its powerful images, the reader now is prepared to exercise on a long chain which meditates on the relation of *praktiké* to knowledge.

The Middle of the Text: A Chain Relating Praktiké *and Knowledge (M 63 to M 72).*   Up to this point in the text the reader has been given proverbs which in various ways reflect on different dimensions of *praktiké*. Now the proverbs become exercises on the relation between this first dimension of the monastic life and its ultimate goal: knowledge. The meditation is proposed in a long chain composed of ten carefully combined proverbs, M 63 to M 72. These ten proverbs numerically form the middle of the text such that the meditation here can be considered as literally the central message of *Ad Monachos*. There is a uniformity in the construction of the chain, each proverb being composed of two lines apiece. In almost each one there is both an expression which refers to *praktiké* and one which refers to knowledge. (M 70 is concerned only with *praktiké* but is balanced by M 71 which refers only to knowledge. M 72 refers exclusively to knowledge as the climax of the chain. In some of the proverbs these expressions are obvious and explicit; in others some biblical symbol is used to refer to one or the other.)

M 63 sets the tone for the chain with a term for *praktiké* and a term for knowledge in the opening line: "Knowledge keeps guard over a monk's way of life." ("Way of life," in Greek πολιτεία, is an Evagrian expression for the monastic practices of *praktiké*.) Yet the second line is concerned to establish a firm link with the preceding proverb on pride: "He who descends from knowledge will fall among thieves." A similarly vivid image of falling is used, and it is observed that pride is one of the main ways in which one falls from knowledge.

M 64 presents a biblical image for knowledge: "From the spiritual rock a river flows." The second line leaves no doubt about the relation to *praktiké*: "The soul accomplished in *praktiké* drinks from it." The biblical language, echoing 1 Corinthians 10:4, evokes a sense of desert wandering, of thirst and hardship, and of thirst being satisfied by the rock who is Christ. Such satisfaction is only for those who have passed through the work of *praktiké*. For those still involved in it, the proverb directs attention toward the goal of knowledge as a source which sustains.

The next two proverbs also speak with a definite biblical language. In M 65 *praktiké*'s terms are the contrast drawn between a pure and an impure soul. "Vessel of election" (cf. Acts 9:15) is the term for knowledge. The first line of the proverb, even leaving a verb out of the construction, could not have expressed the relation between *praktiké* and knowledge any more economically, any more tersely: "A vessel of election, the pure soul." One who has reached the goal of *praktiké*, here described as "pure soul," is virtually the same as one who can enter the realm of knowledge.

Of special interest in the next proverb is the introduction of the term *passionlessness* (ἀπάθεια). As has been noted, this term is virtually synonymous with *praktiké*'s goal.

Thus, the terms for *praktiké* in M 64, 65, and 66 are not simply making vague reference to the life of *praktiké* in general; they are referring far more precisely to its goal. We have seen in this order (in M 64, 65, 66) the terms ψυχή πρακτική, ψυχή καθαρά, and ἀπάθεια. It is from this point in the life of *praktiké*, from the term itself, that the link with knowledge can be made.

M 66 not only introduces the term *passionlessness*, but it likewise opens a unit within the chain made up of three proverbs (M 66, 67, 68) joined together by this term. A close look at the positioning of this chain as well as its content reveals the extraordinary care with which Evagrius joined all the proverbs of *Ad Monachos* into patterns which offer further clues to their fullest meanings. It was already mentioned that the chain M 63 to M 72, which beats away at some length about the relation between *praktiké* and knowledge, is positioned in the middle of the whole collection. Now in M 66 to M 68 we find the center of the center, and we might reasonably expect to find in its center proverb a major clue to the entire text—a proverb which somehow manages or comes close to "saying it all."

M 67 is precisely that. "In front of love, passionless marches;/ in front of knowledge, love." Some readers in the course of their spiritual exercise would have discovered that M 67 is not simply the next proverb to come along but is in fact the middle of the text and holds a clue to the meaning of the entire exercise. The proverb is constructed around three terms: passionlessness, love, and knowledge. The way in which these terms are joined manages to summarize and emphasize some of the most characteristic features of Evagrius' teaching. The word *love* occurs in both lines. In the first line it appears as the goal of *praktiké*. Passionlessness, also a goal in *praktiké*, is not an end in itself. In the second line love is the door to knowledge. Thus, neither is love an end in itself. Knowledge of God is the ultimate goal. In some senses the individual proverbs of the whole text elaborate in various directions this fundamental insight of M 67. It is a center around which the other proverbs are arranged.

Evagrius continues his elaborate construction. M 68 likewise speaks of passionlessness and thus concludes the central unit of M 66 to M 68. But it likewise introduces two more terms which appear together for a first time in this proverb: wisdom and prudence. These two virtues coupled together are interwoven in an upcoming chain, M 123 to M 131, but each of the two virtues is treated singly in the proverbs which immediately follow. M 68 makes it clear that wisdom is a virtue directed toward knowledge, whereas prudence is a virtue which looks toward *praktiké*. "To knowledge, wisdom is added;/ prudence gives birth to passionlessness." This is the way in which Evagrius consistently speaks of these virtues (cf. *Praktikos* 89). Then M 69 and 70 are developments on prudence, while M 71 meditates on wisdom and knowledge.

This intricate chain comes to an especially poetic conclusion with a final proverb based on an allusion to the biblical image of honey as an image for knowledge. This proverb does not make specific mention of *praktiké*. It is as if following the chain through to this point, the reader arrives at the goal of all his striving, the very knowledge of God. This is the last specific mention of knowledge for awhile, and as such then M 72 signals the conclusion of the chain which began with the mention of this same term.

First Block, Section 2: M 73 to M 106

After this intricate and sustained meditation, the next proverb is something like a new start in the text in that it is a fresh invitation to the reader: "Listen, O monk, to the words of your father." In so doing Evagrius imitates a technique used in the biblical book of Proverbs (cf. Prov 4:10; 5:7; 7:1, 24; 8:32–35; etc.). The proverbs which follow until M 106 give a double impression of being at once loosely joined and carefully combined. Perhaps here more than elsewhere in the text does the importance become clear of meditating on each proverb in its own right and not only noticing that it is part of a chain. The details of this arrangement are complex, and they reward more careful analysis than is offered here. However, there is a structural secret to the whole section which is worth observing. The key to uncovering it is already hidden within the first line of M 73, which speaks of "the words of your father." In the center of the proverbs from M 73 to M 106 is a chain composed of five proverbs (M 88 to M 92) whose theme is the monk's spiritual father. Fourteen proverbs precede this chain (M 74 to M 87), and fourteen follow it (M 93 to M 106). There is a coherence in the arrangements in both sets of fourteen, a coherence discovered again by reference to key themes of Evagrius' teaching. Here I limit myself to pointing out just one of the keys in this arrangement.

From M 93 to M 106 the proverbs exercise the various parts of the soul in preparation for the entry into knowledge which occurs at the text's turning point, M 107.

Proverbs exercising first the irascible then the concupiscible part alternate with each other back and forth several times. (The arrangement is complex and, as mentioned, each proverb stands well on its own. This distinguishing of different parts of the soul should not be forced on the text. Perhaps it is best to say that the following proverbs "roughly" are concerned with these parts of the soul: M 94, 95 with the irascible; M 96, 97 with the concupiscible; M 98, 99, 100 with the irascible; M 101, 102, 103 with the concupiscible; M 104 with the irascible.) Then the last two proverbs of the section have to do with the rational part of the soul: "The prudent monk shall be passionless,/ but the imprudent one draws up evils" (M 105). "The wicked eye, the Lord totally blinds;/ but the simple, he will rescue from darkness" (M 106). Both proverbs prepare for the turning point of M 107 in a way that is perhaps inauspicious but nonetheless precisely formulated according to Evagrius' understanding of what is necessary to reach knowledge. Prudence is virtue in the rational part of the soul. It must be established there for the mind to turn itself to knowledge (for it is the rational part of the soul which is used for knowledge) by means of another virtue in that part of the soul, wisdom. A monk must be passionless to enter into knowledge.

As the next proverb begins the whole text's increasing emphasis on knowledge, it does so with a beautiful image of light: the morning star in heaven. It is this morning star which rescues from darkness. We turn now to that proverb, which I have called the text's turning point.

Second Block: M 107 to M 136

Beginning with M 107 the proverbs of *Ad Monachos* sustain a concern with knowledge which carries through to the very end of the text. The issue of knowledge has been present from the start, but heretofore in the text it was joined to other issues of the life of *praktiké*; it was a part of other chains; it was something pointed toward. Now knowledge itself (and various expressions for its different levels) is the main structural component of the chains. As noticed in observing the structure of previous portions of the text, the tightness of the identified chains varies from "quite tight" to "fairly loose," with intermediary levels between these two poles. The same can be said for this portion of the text. Some of the proverbs are extraordinarily suggestive and beautiful. In their individual power they bear out the importance of meditating on them one at a time. Yet here too, as before, there is a richer meaning which emerges when the placement of the proverbs is noticed and meditated upon as well. The comments which follow focus on this aspect of the text, attempting to determine the movement of the whole.

M 107 *as the Turning Point.* M 107 reads, "Like a morning star in heaven and a palm tree in paradise,/ so a pure mind in a gentle soul." Turning point is a strong expression. Is it justified for describing what happens at M 107? Again, at first glance, perhaps not. Certainly the structure at this point in the text is not so immediately evident as was seen in a more tightly constructed chain, as for example in M 63 to M 72. M 107 is a seemingly simple (if slightly more poetic than usual) proverb of only two lines which perhaps comes upon a reader unawares. Yet when a reader exercises on this proverb and its position, I think the claim that it is a turning point is justified from several different perspectives.

One perspective is structural. Something happens in the text here after which the flavor of the whole is never quite the same. Perhaps the image of a musical symphony can help to clarify what happens in the text at this point. M 107 is like some fine, remarkable, "quick" moment (turn) in the symphony after which it is never quite the same; for a new energy has come into the piece which sustains it to the end. To be sure, the shift is subtle, yet it is nonetheless firm for all that. It is like a sound, an instrument, which enters and is heard before it is noticed entering. Yet once it is there and noticed, it drives the piece forward. Some themes already heard are heard again, but they are heard in a new way, with new, richer variations of the theme. There are some intense moments of remarkable beauty and complexity (M 118–120, M 133, 135), some others of considerable tension and even fear (M 123–131, especially M 126). Yet something is driving the whole forward toward its climax, and the listener is caught up in the drive. Gentleness, love, and right doctrine are leading the mind before the very presence of the Holy Trinity (M 136). This is the turn in the text.

Once this shift is noticed, hindsight reveals another structural element to which attention has already been drawn; namely, the arrangement of two sets of fourteen proverbs (M 74 to M 87 and M 93 to M 106) around a central chain of five proverbs on the spiritual father (M 88 to M 92). Thus, on both sides of M 107 the structural arrangement suggests that something significant is taking place in the text at this point.

The contents of M 107 and the range

of meditation it can evoke also justify label-
ing it a turning point. It is one of the most
beautiful and suggestive proverbs in the collection. First, it should be noticed that the
first line of the proverb (and thus of this
whole new section) presents the reader with
two bright and striking images. Simply from
a poetic point of view, this alone signals
some turn in the text. The bright image of
the morning star is the rescue from darkness
spoken of in M 106. Yet these images are not
simply bright and striking. For Evagrius
both are scriptural images which he uses
with consistency to refer to rational creatures
who adhere to the knowledge for which they
were created. (For morning star see Letter
27; *The Scholion on* Ps 109:3; *Praktikos,* Prologue, 2. For tree as image of rational creatures, see Letter 27; *The Scholion on* Ps 21:7;
The Scholion on Prov 2:17; *Kephalaia Gnostica
V,* 67).

The second line of the proverb speaks
of two important realities, the realities of
which the morning star and the palm tree
are offered as images. They are *mind* and
soul. The language is careful and precise. It
speaks of mind *in* a soul, which is consistent
with Evagrius' understanding of the relation
of these two realities. (For Evagrius the mind
is the most fundamental dimension of the
human being; the soul and the body are the

mind's instruments in this world.) The adjectives for mind and soul are critical. He speaks of a *pure* mind and a *gentle* soul. The mind is what is used for contemplation and knowledge, of which the following proverbs will speak. For contemplation and knowledge the mind must be pure. A human being's mind is found in a soul. That soul must be gentle for the mind to be pure. Thus, here *gentle* serves as the term which summarizes the whole of *praktiké*. Its position here at the text's turning point images the absolutely critical importance of gentleness in the monk's coming to knowledge.

The Flow of Proverbs from M 107 to M 110. Identifying M 107 as the turning point receives confirmation from closer attention to the proverbs which immediately follow. It is worth observing their flow, for one by one they lay out some of the key terminology which Evagrius uses to speak of the realm of knowledge. M 107 presents strong poetic images for the *mind*, the foundational human reality, the principle instrument for knowledge. M 108 speaks of the *wise man*, and wisdom is the virtue whose role it is "to contemplate the reasons for the corporeals and incorporeals." Thus does M 108 also introduce the term *reasons of God* (λόγοι θεοῦ). M 109 offers for meditation two other terms:

knowledge of God and *contemplation* (θεωρία).
Then M 110 uses this terminology to express
the hierarchy in levels of knowledge, focusing
on the supreme value of knowledge of the
Trinity. ''Better is knowledge of the Trinity
than knowledge of the incorporeals,/ and the
contemplation of it better than the reasons
for all the aeons.'' The levels of knowledge
which lead up to knowledge of the Trinity
are the subject of many of the following
proverbs, but the last proverb of the movement, M 136, (M 137 being considered a conclusion to the whole) leaves the reader with
what has been suggested in these opening
four; namely, the mind presented before the
Holy Trinity, shining like the morning star.

*Christ's Role in the Progressive Movement toward
Knowledge (M 118 to M 120).* ''Flesh of
Christ: virtues of *praktiké*;/ he who eats it,
passionless shall he be'' (M 118). ''Blood of
Christ: contemplation of created things;/ he
who drinks it, by it becomes wise'' (M 119).
''Breast of the Lord: knowledge of God;/ he
who rests against it, a theologian shall he
be'' (M 120). This chain seems to be one of
the better known portions of *Ad Monachos*,
and well might it be. It is frequently cited as
an example of the way in which Evagrius di-
vides the monastic life into various levels,
and it is a good text for illustrating that. But

there is much more. These three proverbs are dense with possible directions for meditation. They manage to express with an admirable succinctness so much of Evagrius' teaching, not least of all his teaching about Christ, though this often is left without remark by those who draw attention to this chain to indicate the divisions of the monastic life. Here we can at least observe how the chain itself is constructed.

The proverbs could be described as being carefully and precisely composed and ordered. Virtually every word in each of the proverbs has its exact correspondence in the other two. Thus *flesh of Christ* corresponds to *blood of Christ,* and these together correspond to *breast of the Lord.* Next, *virtues of praktiké* corresponds to *contemplation of created things,* and these together correspond to *knowledge of God.* Then there are the verbs. *Eats* corresponds to *drinks,* and these to *rests against.* Finally, there are the "conditions" which each proverb describes. *Passionless* corresponds to *wise,* and these in turn to *theologian.*

Within the single proverbs a correspondence is likewise established, no less precisely expressed. In each proverb the guiding image is some dimension of the Last Supper scene. In M 118 Christ's flesh is identified with the virtues of *praktiké.* This being established, the second line speaks of the condition one reaches if this flesh (these virtues) is eaten: one becomes passionless, Evagrius' term for the goal of *praktiké*. In M 119 Christ's blood is identified with the contemplation of created things. This being established, the second line speaks of the condition one reaches if this blood (this contemplation) is drunk: one becomes wise, Evagrius' term for this level of contemplation. In M 120 the breast of the Lord is identified with the knowledge of God, that is, with the very highest level of knowledge. This being established, the second line speaks of the condition one reaches if he rests against this breast (this knowledge): one becomes a theologian, Evagrius' term for the goal of all knowledge (cf. *The Chapters on Prayer,* 61).

There is not only correspondence in the terminology of the proverbs; a progress is also marked, a progress expressed with each of the terms. Thus, as Evagrius consistently teaches, the virtues of *praktiké* lead to the contemplation of created things, and this contemplation leads to the knowledge of God. Passionlessness opens the way to wisdom, and this leads on to theology. The movement from flesh to blood to breast or from eating to drinking to resting-against is a movement toward an ever greater intimacy with Christ.

Perhaps no other chain in *Ad Monachos* is as tightly packed as this and so rich with meaning. Perhaps no other proverbs exhibit quite the economy of expression. In three two-line proverbs every major phase of the journey to the knowledge of God is offered for meditation. Each phase is expressed in its most basic terminology. And each phase is placed in the tightest possible relationship with Christ; more specifically, with some particular dimension of the incarnate Lord. The role of Christ is placed squarely in the process from beginning to end. He himself *is* the life of *praktiké*. He himself *is* contemplation. He himself *is* the knowledge of God. The beginning of the monastic life is dependent on Christ. Its final goal is equally dependent upon him, indeed on intimacy with him. The whole timbre of the chain is sounded in a Eucharistic key, which is to say that Evagrius is guided by symbols from the Church's central mystery in his understanding of the role of Christ in his own monastic journey and in that of his fellow monks. The mystery of the Eucharist itself may account for the tight conjunction expressed between Christ and the phases of the monastic life as well as accounting for

the tone of intimacy in which the chain fin-
ishes. Only by resting against the breast of
the Lord can one know God, can one be a
theologian.

Wisdom and Prudence vs. False Knowledge (M 123
to M 131). The next chain, a lengthy one, is
a stinging indictment against false knowledge. It is the longest single chain of the
whole text, containing as well the longest
proverb, M 126. Its length and its position
here in the last major movement of the text,
virtually bringing it to its conclusion, are an
indication of the importance of Evagrius'
warning against false knowledge. The reader
has just completed a meditation on the way
in which "grace from the Lord" (M 122)
leads from the the virtues of *praktiké* to theology. The meditation has been rich, beautiful, dense. Now the reader is warned.
Between *praktiké* and the heights of theology
(here understood as the highest union with
God, no longer involved with any sort of dis-
cursive thinking), there are many ways in
which the monk can go astray. In general,
the first block of the text often warns against
the ways in which one can go astray in the
practice of the virtues. But there are also
false paths in what concerns knowledge, and
the present chain is warning against these.

To examine the movement of this carefully designed chain, it is helpful first to observe that there is an overarching structure to the whole. Recognizing that, it is easier to follow the flow of the proverbs one by one. The central beams around which this chain is built are the partner virtues of prudence and wisdom. M 123 introduces the two terms, devoting one line to wisdom, the other to prudence: "Wisdom knows about the dogmas of the demons;/ prudence tracks down their crafty ways." M 131, the last proverb in the chain, does the same: "The wisdom of the Lord raises up the heart;/ his prudence purifies it." In fact, it is this which enables us to identify the intervening proverbs as a unit. Especially interesting is the occurrence of the two virtues in M 126 in the statement against false teachers which says, "there is no prudence and there is no wisdom in their [false teachers'] teachings." This statement falls in the exact middle of that long proverb, there being seven lines on either side of it. It also falls at the exact middle of the whole chain, counting the total lines of the member proverbs. So, once again it can be said that in a quite literal way the *central* message of this chain is that "there is no prudence and there is no wisdom in their teachings." The structure is a perfect chiasm.

Around these central beams of the structure other specific ideas are made to rest. As already mentioned, M 123 introduces the two terms with which the central message of the chain will be formed, namely, wisdom and prudence. In addition, it introduces the image of demons and speaks about their dogmas and crafty ways. Demons are another key thread to this chain. After being mentioned here, they are designated as "angels of death" in M 125. They can be associated with the "lawless men" of M 126, which also speaks of demons and calls them enemies of the Lord. Actually, various demons specialize in causing particular types of problems. Some cause problems in *praktiké*; others in regard to knowledge in all its various dimensions (cf. *Kephalaia Gnostica* I, 10). Wisdom and prudence must know all about all these demons and the ways they operate. Thus, in M 123 Evagrius begins a chain in which he wishes to speak of false knowledge. He does this by mentioning demons and the two virtues which most protect against the demons, who will be shown, as the chain unfolds, to be the real authors of false knowledge.

M 124 returns to the theme of "fathers," which was developed and located in so central a position above (M 88 to M 92). It speaks of their dogmas and calls them holy, contrasting them thereby with the dogmas of the demons mentioned in M 123. "Do not lay to the side the holy dogmas/ which your fathers have laid down." Then these dogmas of the (monastic) fathers are put in direct relation to baptismal faith, evidence that Evagrius did not think of his and other monastic teachings as anything other than a way of life which develops out of this baptismal faith. "Do not abandon the faith of your baptism." M 125 specifies that the demonic teaching about which he is concerned is heresy. "The teachings of heretics: angels of death." As the next proverb shows, these heretics are those who offer "false knowledge," and such teachers are a very concrete and specific concern for Evagrius, which other of his writings show as well as the other sources we have about Evagrius' life (see, for example, *The Lausiac History,* 38).

M 126 is the longest proverb of the entire collection, and it is a relentlessly sounded warning against such teachers and their false knowledge. Like M 1 and M 73 it begins with the invitation to listen to the advice of the father, yet now the tone is more personal; he says, "listen to *me.*" And at the end of the proverb he refers to his personal experience. Strong words and images are used for these false teachers and their false knowledge. These images are strung together one after another; they give the proverb a momentum; the tension builds in it throughout. From one line to the next this strong vocabulary flows: lawless men, traps, snares, false knowledge, dark teachings, venom of asps, no prudence and no wisdom, evils, enemies, demons, no light. All these images are scriptural, and catching the scriptural allusions expands the meditation (see the index to scriptural allusions).

After this long proverb, the chain completes itself with five more proverbs of two lines apiece. The first of these, M 127, acts as a two-line summary of the fifteen lines of M 126. Having stated his warnings so vividly and at comparative length there, Evagrius can now simply say, "The lying man will fall away from God;/ he who deceives his neighbor will fall into evils." M 128 and M 129 are proverbs which contrast true knowledge with worldly knowledge. With their images of "paradise of God, garden of herbs, river of the Lord, Egyptian wise men," etc., they would likely seem mysterious and strange to someone unacquainted with the way in which Evagrius thinks scripturally; but he expects his reader to be familiar with this procedure and either to recognize the allusions and their meaning or be challenged to find them. By a use of scriptural language Evagrius can evoke much

in a few words. These two proverbs evoke
Deuteronomy 11:10-11, which is meant to
guide and promote the meditation.

   M 130 comes specifically again to the
issue of pride. The allusion here is to the
Lord's own words: "He who exalts himself
will be humbled" (Matt 23:12, cf. M 96).
This dominical saying is applied to the false
teachers spoken of in this chain. Pride, de-
fined in M 62 as saying "Powerful am I,"
in the presence of God, can be a source for
such false teaching. It is a desire to exalt
oneself. The image of being brought low as
if on a wheel is a variation of the falling
away from God mentioned in M 127 and of
the image of being brought low mentioned in
M 62.

   M 131 signals the close of the chain by
its mention again of the virtues of wisdom
and prudence. As they are stated in this
proverb and consistent with how these virtues are discussed in Evagrius, prudence
looks towards *praktiké* and is thus said to *pu-
rify* the heart. Wisdom looks toward knowledge and so is said to *raise* the heart up.

*Various Levels of Knowledge Leading to the Holy
Trinity (M 132 to M 136).*   After this long and
perhaps even tiring exercise on true and false
knowledge, the whole exercise comes to a
quiet close with five simple, rich proverbs of

two lines apiece, each of which repeats for one final time some point related to various levels and terms for knowledge which have appeared elsewhere in the text.

M 132, after the diatribe on false knowledge, seems now willingly to admit that true knowledge is not an easy thing to reach, not only because of false teachers but because of the difficult and mysterious nature of the questions themselves. Yet though these be hard to understand, the proverb also offers a promise: ''The reasons of providence are dark, and hard for the mind (δυσνόητοι) are the contemplations of the judgment;/ but the man accomplished in *praktiké* will know them.'' Thus, as the text comes to its conclusion, it repeats here a theme which was located literally in the center of the text (M 63 to M 72); namely, the relation between *praktiké* and knowledge.

M 133 builds on this theme of *praktiké* in talk particularly suited to its goal as it speaks of purifying oneself. And then unable, it seems, to resist saying it one last time, Evagrius comes back to gentleness and its relation to knowledge. ''He who purifies himself will see intelligible natures;/ reasons of incorporeals, a gentle monk will know.'' (Here ''intelligible natures'' refers to seeing the nature of the original creation of beings who were made to know God.) The turning

point in the text at M 107 turned on the issue of gentleness. The first specific development after the proverbs which presented
some of the basic terminology (M 107 to
M 110) concerned itself with gentleness (M 111
to M 114). The theme has been touched upon
at regular points throughout the whole text.
And now the text concludes with one final
mention of it. The construction of the Greek
text forms a chiasm (roughly possible to follow in the English) in which ''intelligible natures'' and ''reasons of the incorporeals'' lie
immediately side by side, sandwiched between the first and last words of the proverb:
''purifies himself ($\varkappa\alpha\theta\alpha\iota\varrho\omega\nu$ $\dot{\epsilon}\alpha\nu\tau\dot{\delta}\nu$)'' and
''gentle monk ($\mu o\nu\alpha\chi\dot{o}\varsigma$ $\pi\varrho\alpha\tilde{\nu}\varsigma$).'' It is as if to
say that gentleness and purity must always
surround knowledge.

M 134 is a proverb directed against
two specific doctrinal errors, such as would
have been the reference in the previous chain
on false knowledge. It is not surprising that
Evagrius should place a proverb like this toward the end of his text. If he thinks it
generally important to follow the teachings of
the fathers and the Church, ''this should be
especially observed concerning the Holy
Trinity'' (*Scholia on Proverbs,* 22:28).

M 135 offers the striking image of the
heart growing larger under the influence of
the various contemplations. ''Contemplations

of worlds enlarge the heart;/ reasons of providence and judgment lift it up." The reasons of providence and judgment, that is, knowing the why of God's creations and his intricate plan of salvation—these lift the heart up. When the reader savors the proverb by lingering with it some time, the sense it offers is one of a wonderful expansiveness. Worlds (κόσμοι) and contemplations (θεωρίαι) and reasons (λόγοι) are all in the plural. These seem to invade the heart and in their greatness cause it to grow wider so that the meaning can be contained there. The movement in this invasion is ever upward.

In M 136 this raised up heart is now named *mind,* the original creation and the definitive object of salvation. The other levels of knowledge, the lesser contemplations, raise the mind to its last and greatest goal, the Holy Trinity itself. Of the Trinity, Evagrius is here characteristically lacking in details and silent, content but to mention it. But the proverb and the whole collection end with a sense of openness before a great mystery. In the course of 136 proverbs the reader has circled and climbed through many levels of *praktiké*, passed by dangerous demons, and heard of wonderful and mysterious contemplations. There has been a continual movement upward in the meditation. But at the summit of the climb, the reader is left now

with a sense of things just beginning. The
mind is presented before the Holy Trinity.
And what might that mean!

Conclusion

I have tried to comment on the structure of *Ad Monachos* with something of the
spirit which enables the structure to be
uncovered: by treating the text as a spiritual
exercise. As disciples familiar with the terminology and concepts of Evagrius' monastic
teachings worked with these proverbs one by
one, they could not have failed to recognize
that in them they had been given various
"words" from a father and that these words
could exercise a disciple in all the major
dimensions of the spiritual life. The exercise
is in no way haphazard. Indeed, working
one by one with the proverbs in the order
presented, a disciple is led slowly upward toward the goal of all spiritual striving: knowledge of the Trinity. But the disciple is made
to travel by the only way which, according
to Evagrius, leads there; namely, the ardu-
ous and seemingly circuitous path of exercising love and temperance and related virtues
again and again, by the dangerous roads
which pass by the snares of many wily demons. For one who truly exercises, the

words of this father are challenging and rough, and yet their central concern keeps attention fixed on knowledge, a goal sweeter than honey, bright like the morning star, beautiful as the palm tree in paradise. Love is the sure path to such knowledge, love expressed most especially as gentleness. Prudence and wisdom are the antidote to the venom of false knowledge. By exercising these virtues, the mind in its present condition is raised up to seeing correctly the reason with which God made the world, both the corporeal world and the incorporeal world. When the mind understands that in its deepest sense it is made in the image of the incorporeal God, then it is ready to know this God, one and three, in whose image it is made.

Ad Monachos is a spiritual exercise which offers its reader the guide whereby the mind comes to the knowledge for which it was made. Hadot argues that it is impossible to understand ancient philosophy without taking into account the concrete perspectives and existential attitude upon which its dogmatic edifice is constructed. The same holds true for Evagrius. His writings are exercises in learning to live, learning to die, learning to love, learning to know God. If the concrete perspective in which he conceived these lessons is overlooked, then his dogmatic edifice appears perhaps esoteric, perhaps heretical, or perhaps just simply strange. *Ad Monachos* is a text which helps us to taste the existential concern with which Evagrius proffered his teachings, and it traces this concern through every major dimension of the spiritual journey as he conceived it. For this reason I think that as interest in Evagrius continues to grow, it is a text which must require the close attention both of scholars and those who would use his thought for their own spiritual guidance.

This edition of *Ad Monachos* has been prepared in a format which will promote meditation on the proverbs. Even as the structure of the whole is more and more discerned, still the proverbs need to be meditated upon and practiced one by one. The scriptural citations and allusions need to be recognized and the meditation of each proverb expanded in the light of the scriptural text. This process, followed over many years, has been found by previous generations of monks to lead to knowledge of the Holy Trinity. It is hoped that this same road map might prove useful again in our own day.

Index to Scriptural
Citations and Allusions

The task of making a scriptural index to *Ad Monachos* presents some difficult decisions for the compiler. In some cases a proverb will clearly be seen to be citing directly or almost directly a particular passage in Scripture. In many other instances the language of the Evagrian text is so saturated with the language of Scripture that it is difficult to identify with certainty a particular scriptural text as the inspiration for the language of Evagrius' proverb.

The following index seeks to distinguish between these various ways in which Evagrius lets himself be inspired by the Scriptures. It offers first scriptural texts which are direct or near direct citations of Scripture. These are designated by the signal (C) (meaning "close") after the scriptural

reference. Other references are to scriptural
verses which are in the same general direc-
tion as the proverb in question, either from
the point of view of vocabulary or from a
theological position expressed. The scope
here is not to claim that in every case
Evagrius would have had these scriptural
passages in mind, though I have tried not to
stray far from collecting texts which seem to
be his actual inspiration.

The scope, however, is to indicate, on
the one hand, the extent to which Evagrius'
thinking is shaped by the language of the
Scripture and, on the other hand, to indicate
the kind of passages that are brought to the
mind of a meditating monk who, knowing
the Scriptures well, receives Evagrius' proverb for his meditation. In some cases it is
useful to take a single word from the
Evagrian proverb and indicate the extent of
its use in Scripture. Where a particular
Greek term is important, it is indicated with
the reference. Otherwise, the word on which
the reference is based is given in English.
Yet in every case, of course, it has been the
Greek text which has been consulted. Some
of the references are to the whole Evagrian
proverb; others are to a particular line or
even a phrase within the line. These latter
are indicated by reference to the line by the
letters **a, b, c,** (in bold), etc. referring

respectively to the first, second, third line, etc. of a proverb.

Finally, when a citation or allusion to a passage from the Psalms or the book of Proverbs is commented on by Evagrius in his scholia on the Psalms or Proverbs in a way which sheds light on the proverb from *Ad Monachos*, such references are followed by the designation (*). In short, the index which follows cannot be presented in a particularly "neat" fashion; and yet, I think it is the kind of index required by the nature of the text under examination. Pages of numbers are not especially inspiring for a reader, yet I would urge the one who wishes to understand the spirit of *Ad Monachos* well not to neglect to meditate on its proverbs inside the scriptural world in which it means to stand. This index is offered as a help toward that end.

M 1. Prov 1:1-2; 5-6 (C); Sir 18:29; Rom 8:16-17 (C). *ἀκούειν:* LXX makes very frequent use of the term, especially in Wisdom literature, where it is a classical beginning to an exhortation. See below, references at M 73. *Inheritance:* Ps 15:5; 36:18; 60:6; 93:5; 134:12; Matt 25:34.

M 2. Luke 11:11-13; Heb 12:7 (C). *ἀπόλλειν:* frequent in Proverbs (LXX) for loosing the fruits of good works.

M 3. For relation of faith to *praktiké*, see 2 Chr 34:12; Prov 15:27, 28. Faith and gentleness: Sir 1:26. Faith and knowledge: Sir 46:15; Eph 4:13. Love and knowledge: Col 2:2-3. Love and faith: 1 Tim 1:5. Add virtue to faith: 2 Pet 1:5. For knowledge as faith's goal based on biblical texts, see Evagrius in Ps 85:11; 94:11; 137:5; Prov 4:10.

M 4. Prov 1:7 (*) and parallels; Ps 110:10. ἐγκράτεια ψυχῆς: Sir 18:15, 30.

M 5. Rom 5:3-5 (C); Jas 1:3-4; Ps 129:4-6. **b.** John 17:10; Rom 8:30; Ps 90:15.

M 6. a. 1 Cor 9:27 (C). **b.** Rom 13:14 as in TP 53; Eph 5:29.

M 7. Mark 7:21; Rom 1:29; 1 Cor 6:18; Gal 5:19; Col 3:5. Faith, love, holiness, chastity: 2 Tim 2:15.

M 8. Jesus and withdrawal: John 6:15. Purity of heart: Matt 5:8; Ps 23:4. Love from a pure heart, a good conscience, and sincere faith: 1 Tim 1:5. Love and purity: 1 Pet 1:22; 2 Tim 2:22. ταράσσειν: very frequent in LXX; in NT see Mark 6:50; John 11:33; Acts 15:24.

M 9. "Better A than B" is a frequent structure in Proverbs: see 8:1; 15:16, 17, 29; 16:19, 32; 17:1; 19:22; 21:9, 19; 22:1; 24:5; 25:24; 27:5, 10; 28:6; 29:1.

M 10. Comparisons constructed with ὁμοίως, ὡς, ὥσπερ, ὅν τρόπον are frequent in Proverbs, as for example, Prov 10:26; 11:22; 19:12; 21:1; 24:30-31; 25:11-26; 31:14. μνησικακεῖν: Ezek 25:12; Zech 7:10. **b.** chaff: Matt 3:12.

M 11. Prov 3:24 (*). **a.** Sir 37:30. **b.** Sir 31:20; Wis 18:17. **c.** Joel 1:19; same image, though use of image is different.

M 12. Prov 3:24-25 (*); Prov 13:3. "Terrified" in eschatological sense: Luke 21:9; 1 Pet 3:5. "Terrified" used with θύμος: Isa 31:4. "Terrified" is frequent in LXX in phrases like "Do not be afraid"; often used together with φοβεῖν. "Without fear": Prov 1:33; 3:24-25 (*); 19:3; Luke 1:74. πραΰς: Num 12:3; Job 36:15; Ps 24:9; 33:2; 36:11 (with κληρονομήσουνι); 75:9; 146:6; 149:4; Sir 3:18; 10:15; Isa 26:6; Zeph 3:12; Zech 9:9; Matt 5:5; 11:29 (with ταπεινός); 21:5 (citing Zech 9:9); 1 Pet 3:4. πραΰτης: Ps 44:4 (with truth and righteouness); 131:1; Sir 1:26; 3:17; 4:8; 10:28; 45:4 (with πίστις concerning Moses); Gal 5:23 (in a list of fruits of the Spirit); Eph 4:2 (with ταπεινοφροσύνη, μακροθυμία, ἀγάπη); Col 3:12-13 (with other virtues, including μακροθυμία); 1 Tim 6:11 (with other virtues); 2 Tim 2:25 (with other virtues and with the verb παιδεύειν); Titus 3:2; Jas 1:21; 3:13 (connected with wisdom); 1 Pet 3:16.

M 13. Prov 25:23 (*); ἄνεμος used in Synoptic accounts of storms at sea. μνησικακία: Prov 12:28; 21:24; Zech 7:10; Ezek 25:12. **a.** Jude 12.

M 14. Matt 5:44; Luke 6:28. "To spare the tongue": Job 7:11; 42:3 (same expression; different use); Prov 10:19; 17:27; Wis 1:11. "Sadden neighbor": Deut 15:10; Sir 3:12; 4:2; Tob 4:3; 10:13.

M 15. Prov 15:1; 21:14 (*); 25:21; Matt 5:24; Rom 12:17-21; Eph 4:25. **a.** 1 Cor 13:5. **b.** Gen 29:13; 43:17 (C). **d.** Judg 19:10. Prov 17:1; 23:7. **e.** ῥύεσθαι very frequent in LXX and also common in NT. For "deliver soul" see Job 33:30; Ps 6:4; 16:13; 21:20; 32:19; 55:13; 56:4; 85:13; 88:48; 114:4; 119:2; Prov 14:25; 22:23; 23:14; Ezek 3:19, 21; 14:20; 33:9. **f.** πρόσκομμα: Sir 17:25; 34:16; 39:24; Rom 14:13; 1 Cor 8:9.

M 16. Matt 5:3; Luke 6:20; Rom 12:9-16; Phil 4:4; 1 Thess 5:16; 1 Pet 4:13.

M 17. Matt 19:23-26 (C); Mark 10:23-27 (C); Luke 18:24-28 (C).

M 18. **a.** φιλάργυρος: 1 Tim 6:10; 2 Tim 3:2; Sir 31:5. **b.** Ps 38:6. Eccl 2:8. Zech 9:3. σκοτίζειν: Ps 68:23; Isa 13:10; Matt 24:29; Mark 13:24; Luke 23:45; Rom 1:21; 11:10; Eph 4:18; Rev 8:12; 9:2. συνάγειν with other negative things: Ps 40:6; Prov 10:10; Mic 1:7; Hag 1:6.

M 19. For the general tone see Num 24:5-6; Ps 14; 1; Pet 5:5. Contrast of humble and proud is frequent in LXX and NT. αὐλίζειν: frequent in LXX, as for example in Ps 24:13; 80:1; Sir 24:7;

51:23. ἀρά: frequent in LXX, but in NT only at Rom 3:14.

M 20. παραβαίνειν is frequent in LXX with "commands," "words," "ways," "law." Likewise for φυλάσσειν.

M 21. Rom 6:3-11; 2 Cor 4:10; Gal 2:19-20; Col 2:12-13; 2 Tim 2:11; 1 Pet 2:24. **a.** ζηλόω is not used with "Christ" in NT, but here the sense seems to be "imitate" as in 1 Cor 4:16; 11:1; 2 Cor 4:10; Phil 3:10; Col 3:3. μακάριος: frequent in LXX and very frequent in NT. **b.** Rom 6:3-11. **c.** Rom 6:12, 19; Gal 5:19-21. **d.** Comparisons constructed with ὁμοιός, ὡς, ὥσπερ, ὅν τρόπον are frequent in Proverbs, as for example, Prov 10:26; 11:22; 19:12; 21:1; 24:30-31; 25:11-26; 31:14.

M 22. **a.** οὐαί: very frequent in Isa and Jer. ἄνομος: very frequent in LXX; also 2 Thess 2:8. "Day of death" and similar: Eccl 8:8; John 12:48. **b.** "Perish": used frequently in Proverbs as in Prov 11:7; together with "woe": Jer 31:1. **c.** crow: Isa 34:11; Prov 30:17 (*). **c, d.** Prov 27:8 (*).

M 23. **a.** ὁδηγεῖν: for Exodus in Exod 15:13; Neh 9:12; see also Ps 22:3; 26:11; Wis 10:10. The verb is used frequently in the Psalms, usually with God as subject. Here angels are intermediaries.

M 24. **a.** Prov 11:2 (C). **b.** Ps 15:10; 96:10 (with souls); Prov 22:11. "Holy ones": frequent in LXX.

M 25. The sense of this proverb is found frequently in Proverbs; see especially Prov 27:4 and also Wis 19:1; Eccl 5:9; Sir 22:23; Matt 19:21 (C). **a.** ἀνελεήμων: Rom 1:31; Jas 1:6. **b.** "Treasure": in NT frequently associated with kingdom of heaven, as for example, Matt 13:44; 25:34-35 (used together with "inherit"); see below references at M 87.

M 26. Sir 10:30; Heb 11:26.

M 27. Sir 6:30; 21:21; 22:17; 2 Tim 4:8.

M 28. The sense is expressed frequently in Proverbs; see also Matt 10:9.

M 29. **a.** "Inherit": very frequent in LXX, as for example Ps 36:29; Isa 61:7-8. Also frequent in NT with some expression for salvation as object, as in 1 Cor 6:9, 10; 15:50. **b.** Matt 6:26; Luke 12:24; Rev 12:6, 14. "Holy ones": frequent in LXX.

M 30. **a.** Prov 14:21, 31; 19:22; 22:9; Ps 111:9; Sir 4:8; 2 Cor 9:9; **b.** "Filled (πιμπλάναι) with good things": Ps 64:4, 11; 103:28; 125:2; Prov 15:4; Eccl 6:3; Sir 22:23; 37:24; 42:25; 48:12; Isa 27:6; Jer 27:19; 51:17. πιμπλάναι used in NT with Holy Spirit at Luke 1:15, 41, 67; Acts 2:4; 4:8, 31; 9:17; 13:9. Compare M 94, M 115.

M 31.   a. ἀναπαύειν: Prov 21:20 (*); Ps 94:11 (*);
Matt 11:28-29 (C). For gentle, see above at M 12.
b. Ps 9:5 (*); 17:7 (*); 46:9 (*); Prov 12:23; 25:5
(*); 28:22 (*).

M 32.   Prov 14:22. μισθός: used in NT as
reward for the kingdom, as in Matt 5:12; 20:8;
1 Cor 3:8; see also Wis 10:17; Sir 51:30; Eccl 4:9.

M 33.   Ps 9:15 (C); 30:4; 34:8; 56:6; 63:5; 118:110;
139:5; 141:3; Prov 6:2; 12:13; 18:7; Eccl 10:8.

M 34.   "Better A than B" is a frequent
structure in Proverbs: see 8:1; 15:16, 17, 29; 16:19,
32; 17:1; 19:22; 21:9, 19; 22:1; 24:5; 25:24; 27:5, 10;
28:6; 29:1.

M 35.   Matt 12:30 (C); Luke 11:23 (C).

M 36.   Comparisons constructed with ὅμοιός,
ὡς, ὥσπερ, ὅν τρόπον are frequent in Proverbs, as
for example, Prov 10:26; 11:22; 19:12; 21:1; 24:30-31;
25:11-26; 31:14.

M 37.   Matt 26:41; Luke 22:40, 46; Eph 6:18;
1 Thess 5:17. For διαλογισμοί and heart: Matt
15:19; Luke 2:35; 5:22; 6:8; 9:46-47; 24:38.

M 38.   Prov 12:11; 20:1 (*); 23:20, 30 (*); Ps
104:33 (*). "Wine gladdens" (in positive sense):
Ps 103:15; Sir 40:20; Eccl 10:19.

M 39.

M 40. "Pasch": very frequent in LXX. "Pentecost": Acts 2:1.

M 41. **b.** μνησικακία: Prov 12:28; 21:24; Zech 7:10; Ezek 25:12.

M 42. **b.** "Hate brother": 1 John 2:9, 11; 3:15; 4:20. "Mighty fall": Job 18:12; 20:5; 37:16; Jdt 8:19.

M 43. 1 Tim 2:4; 6:20. **b.** προσέχειν: 1 Tim 1:4; 4:1; 6:3; Titus 1:4. "End shamefully": Prov 15:10 (C) (*).

M 44. "Better A than B" is a frequent structure in Proverbs; see 8:1; 15:16, 17, 29; 16:19, 32; 17:1; 19:22; 21:9, 19; 22:1; 24:5; 25:24; 27:5, 10; 28:6; 29:1. For content see Prov 15:17; 17:1. **b.** "impurity of soul": Prov 6:16 (C).

M 45. Comparisons constructed with ὅμοιός, ὡς, ὥσπερ, ὅν τρόπον are frequent in Proverbs, as for example, Prov 10:26; 11:22; 19:12; 21:1; 24:30-31; 25:11-26; 31:14. **a.** διαφθείρειν: frequently used in LXX for enemies. **b.** Ps 136:9 (C).

M 46. For the whole chain of M 46 to M 52 see Matt 26:36-46, especially v. 41. Comparisons constructed with ὅμοιός, ὡς, ὥσπερ, ὅν τρόπον are frequent in Proverbs, as for example, Prov 10:26; 11:22; 19:12; 21:1; 24:30-31; 25:11-26; 31:14. **b.** Ps 101:8 (C) (*); Prov 31:15 (*).

M 47. **b.** "μὴ ἀπώσῃ": Prov 1:8; 6:20; 16:3. **c.** Prov 5:21; 15:3. **d.** Job 10:14; Sir 7:8; 11:10.

M 48. Prov 6:4 (*), 10; Sir 31:20.

M 49. Prov 6:4 (*), 10; Sir 31:20.

M 50. **a.** Ps 67:2; Isa 64:1.

M 51. "Better A than B" is a frequent structure in Proverbs; see 8:1; 15:16, 17, 29; 16:19, 32; 17:1; 19:22; 21:9, 19; 22:1; 24:5; 25:24; 27:5, 10; 28:6; 29:1. **b.** "Impurity of soul": Prov 6:16 (C).

M 52. **a.** Ps 126:2; Prov 12:25; Jer 31:26. **b.** Prov 4:16 (*); Sir 31:2; 40:5.

M 53. Matt 23:12; 1 Pet 5:6. **a.** μετάνοια: Matt 3:2; 4:17. ἀνορθοῦν: used for throne in 2 Kgs and 1 Chr; Ps 17:35 (with παιδεία); Ps 144:14; 145:8; Sir 11:12. **b.** στηρίζειν: frequently used in LXX with heart. For gentle, see above at M 12.

M 54. For M 54 to M 56 see Ps 142:3-6; Sir 38:20-21. **a.** μιμνήσκεσθαι: very frequent in LXX. ἔξοδος: very frequent in LXX; see also 2 Pet 1:15. **b.** κρίσις: frequent both in LXX and NT. **c.** πλημμέλεια: frequent in LXX, especially in Lev.

M 55. Comparisons constructed with ὁμοιός, ὡς, ὥσπερ, ὃν τρόπον are frequent in Proverbs, as for example, Prov 10:26; 11:22; 19:12; 21:1; 24:30-31; 25:11-26; 31:14. **a.** Eccl 10:4 (C); Ps 118:28. "Spirit of listlessness": Isa 61:3. **c.** Eph 6:12. **d.** Prov 17:3.

M 56. Sir 30:21, 23; 38:19-21; Luke 22:45-46; 2 Cor 7:10.

M 57. Sir 5:1, 8; Matt 6:25; Mark 10:23; 1 Cor 7:32-34a. **a.** μεριμνᾶν: Matt 6:25-34; Luke 10:41; 12:22-34; 1 Cor 7:32-34a; Phil 4:6. **b.** πενθεῖν: Luke 6:25 πικρῶς: Matt 26:75.

M 58. Prov 6:27, 28 (*). σκορπίος: Deut 8:15; Luke 10:19.

M 59. **a.** ὄφις: Gen 3:1; Ps 57:4; 139:3; Wis 16:5; Sir 21:2; Luke 10:19; 1 Cor 10:9; 2 Cor 11:3; Rev 12:9; 20:2. **b.** ὠδίνειν: Ps 7:14; Sir 34:5. λογισμός is frequent in LXX. For λογισμός with heart, see Prov 19:21.

M 60. Ps 16:3; 25:2; 65:10; 67:30; 138:1, 23; Prov 17:3 (C); Sir 2:5; 31:6; Wis 3:6; Jer 9:7; 11:20; 12:3; 17:10; 20:2; Zech 13:9.

M 61. **a.** περίελε σεαυτοῦ: Prov 4:24. **c, d.** Jas 4:1-3.

M 62. Prov 3:24; Sir 10:7, 9, 12, 13, 18; Matt 23:12; Luke 14:11; 18:14. **b.** Isa 14:12-17; Ezek 28:6, 17. The opposite: Ps 88:8; Jas 4:10; 1 Pet 5:6. **c.** Ps 15:10; 21:1; 70:9-11; Jer 12:7. **d.** Prov 29:23 (*). **e.** πτοεῖν: frequent in LXX, as in Prov 3:25 (*). **f.** Wis 17:21.

M 63. **a.** φυλάσσειν (here διαφυλάσσειν): very frequent in LXX. **b.** Luke 10:30 (C).

M 64. John 7:38; 1 Cor 10:4.

M 65. **a.** Acts 9:15 (C); 2 Tim 2:21-22. **b.** Eph 4:31; πίμπλημι with something evil: Gen 6:11, 13;

Jer 28:5; Ezek 8:17; 9:9; Ps 87:3; Prov 1:31; 12:21; Sir 23:11.

M 66. **a.** 1 Cor 3:1-3; Heb 5:12-14; 1 Pet 2:1-2. **b.** ὑψοῦν: very frequent in Psalms for salvation.

M 67.

M 68. Prov 2:6; 8:12; Eccl 1:16, 17, 18; 2:21, 26; 7:13; 9:10; Wis 6:22; Rom 11:33; Col 2:3; wisdom and prudence: Eph 1:8. **b.** τίκτειν: Prov 10:23 with wisdom and prudence.

M 69.

M 70. Ps 10:3; 56:4; 63:7; 90:5; Eph 6:16.

M 71. **a.** Eph 4:30-32. **b.** χείλη δόλια, etc.: Ps 11:2, 3; 16:1; 30:18; 51:4; 108:2; 119:2, 3. δόλιος: Ps 5:6; 42:1; Prov 12:6; 13:9, 13.

M 72. Ps 18:11; 80:17; 118:103; Prov 16:24; 24:13 (*); 27:7 (*).

M 73. **a.** New beginnings with invitation to listen frequent in Proverbs, as in Prov 4:10; 5:7; 7:1, 24; 8:32-35; 22:17-18 (*); 23:19, 22-26. **b.** Prov 5:7 (C). **c.** Prov 6:22 (C).

M 74. **a.** ἐκθλίψει ψυχάς: Prov 12:13; Sir 40:14. **b.** μνησικακία: Prov 12:28; 21:24; Zech 7:10; Ezek 25:12.

M 75. **a.** Luke 16:1ff (C). **b.** Prov 11:21 (C) (*); 19:5 (C), 9 (C); 28:20 (C).

M 76. Ps 111:5; Luke 12:42; 16:8; Acts 2:45; 1 Cor 4:1-2; Titus 1:7; 1 Pet 4:10.

M 77. **a.** ἐξολεθρεύειν: very frequent in LXX. **b.** Prov 20:20; Matt 25:26.

M 78. Ps 36:21; 111:5. Prov 12:10; 13:9, 11; 21:26. "Better A than B" is a frequent structure in Proverbs; see 8:1; 15:16, 17, 29; 16:19, 32; 17:1; 19:22; 21:9, 19; 22:1; 24:5; 25:24; 27:5, 10; 28:6; 29:1.

M 79. ἄφρων contrasted with φρόνιμος: Prov 10:23-24; 17:10; 19:25.

M 80.

M 81. **a.** μελετᾶν: This is what the just man does with the Law, frequent in Proverbs and in Psalms. For negative: Prov 19:27 (C) (*); 24:2; Isa 59:3, 13. **b.** παραλογίζεσθαι: Col 2:4; Jas 1:22.

M 82. Matt 6:25. **a.** "Fills his stomach": Job 20:23. **b.** ποιμαίνειν: Prov 28:7 (*); 29:3 (*). **c.** Prov 3:32.

M 83. **a.** Prov 5:3 (*). **b.** Prov 9:18a (*). **c, d.** Comparisons constructed with ὅμοιός, ὡς, ὥσπερ, ὅν τρόπον are frequent in Proverbs as for example, Prov 10:26; 11:22; 19:12; 21:1; 24:30-31; 25:11-26; 31:14.

M 84. 1 Cor 13:5-6.

M 85.   **a.** For gentle, see above at M 12. **b.**
ἀπωθεῖν: frequent in LXX with Lord as subject.

M 86.   Prov 22:13 (C) (*); Sir 10:5.

M 87.   Prov 18:19; 2 Cor 1:4; 2:7. **c.** Ps 15:9;
72:21; 85:11; Prov 15:13; 17:22; 23:15; 27:11. **d.**
"Treasure in heaven": Matt 6:20; 19:21; Mark
10:21; Luke 12:33; 18:22.

M 88.   Prov 6:20; 19:13, 27 (*); 20:20, 29.

M 89.   Prov 6:19 (*); 18:1 (C) (*).

M 90.   **d.** "Book of the living": Ps 68:28; Phil
4:3; Rev 3:5; 13:8; 20:15; 22:19.

M 91.   Prov 13:1; 15:5, 32; 19:8. **b.** ἐμπίπτειν εἰς
κακά: Prov 13:7; 17:16 (*), 20 (*); 28:14.

M 92.   **a.** μακάριος: frequent in LXX and very
frequent in NT. φυλάσσειν: very frequent in
LXX. **b.** διατηρεῖν: frequent in LXX.

M 93.   **a.** ζημιοῦν: Prov 19:19 (C) (*); 21:11; 22:3;
Matt 16:26.

M 94.   **a.** Prov 3:6 (C); 4:24; 11:5 (C); Jas 3:5-12.
b. Prov 4:23. (C) "Filled (πιμπλάναι) with good
things": Ps 64:4, 11; 103:28; 125:2; Prov 15:4; Eccl
6:3; Sir 22:23; 37:24; 42:25; 48:12; Isa 27:6; Jer
27:19; 51:17. πιμπλάναι used in NT with Holy
Spirit at Luke 1:15, 41, 67; Acts 2:4; 4:8, 31; 9:17;
13:9. Compare M 30, M 115.

M 95. **a.** Prov 11:13 (C); Sir 5:9, 14; 6:1; 28:13.
b. Prov 11:12 (C).

M 96. **a.** πείθειν: Prov 11:28 (C); 14:6; frequent
in Psalms with Lord; frequent in LXX with
idols; Luke 18:9 (C), thus connected with second
line of M 96 and Luke 18:14. **b.** Matt 18:4; 23:12;
Luke 14:11; 18:14.

M 97. **a.** "Trough of the stomach": Prov 25:15
(*). **b.** Prov 6:4 (*), 9 (*). **d.** Luke 1:35 (C).

M 98. Prov 15:18; 19:11 (*). ἡσυχάζειν: used
frequently in LXX with "land" or "city" as
subject.

M 99. For gentle, see above at M 12.

M 100. Prov 16:19; Sir 2:4; Matt 18:4; 23:12;
Luke 1:48, 52; 14:11; 18:14; Jas 1:9. **b.** ὑψοῦν:
frequent as word for salvation in LXX, especially
in Psalms.

M 101. **a.** λαμπτήρ σβεσθήσεται: Prov 20:20 (C);
24:20 (C). "Track down banquets": Prov 23:30
(C). **b.** Prov 20:20.

M 102. Matt 12:43. **a.** Ezek 4:10-11 (C). **b.** 1 Cor
6:18.

M 103. **a.** Matt 25:31-46. **b.** Prov 5:11 (C) (*);
1 Cor 9:27.

M 104. Prov 17:5; 24:17-18 (C) (*). **c.** Ps 138:23;
Prov 15:11; 24:12; Acts 1:24; 15:8. **d.** παραδιδόναι:

very common in this sense in LXX, as in Prov 6:1 (*); see also Rom 1:24, 26, 28; 1 Cor 5:5.

M 105. ἄφρων contrasted with φρόνιμος: Prov 10:23-24; 17:10; 19:25. **b.** "Draw up evils": Prov 20:5.

M 106. Matt 6:22-23 (C).

M 107. Comparisons constructed with ὅμοιός, ὡς, ὥσπερ, ὅν τρόπον are frequent in Proverbs as for example, Prov 10:26; 11:22; 19:12; 21:1; 24:30-31; 25:11-26; 31:14. **a.** "Morning star": Job 3:9; 11:17 with verse 13; 41:9; Isa 14:12; Ps 109:3 (*); Luke 1:78; 2 Pet 1:19; Rev 2:28; 22:16. Tree: Ps 91:12-15 (*); Prov 3:18 (*); 11:30 (*); Ezek 17:24; 40:16-37; 41:18-25. **b.** For gentle, see above at M 12.

M 108. **a.** John 5:39; 1 Cor 2:10; 1 Pet 1:11 **b.** "Mocks them": Prov 30:17 (*).

M 109. Comparisons constructed with ὅμοιός, ὡς, ὥσπερ, ὅν τρόπον are frequent in Proverbs as for example, Prov 10:26; 11:22; 19:12; 21:1; 24:30-31; 25:11-26; 31:14. **a.** Hate: Prov 1:22, 29; 5:12. **b.** Ps 36:15.

M 110. "Better A than B" is a frequent structure in Proverbs; see 8:1; 15:16, 17, 29; 16:19, 32; 17:1; 19:22; 21:9, 19; 22:1; 24:5; 25:24; 27:5, 10; 28:6; 29:1. **b.** αἰών: very frequent in NT; see also Ps 144:13 (*).

M 111. **a.** Grey: Prov 20:29; Sir 6:18; 25:4; Wis 4:9. For gentle, see above at M 12. **b.** 1 Tim 2:4.

M 112. Isa 57:15; Ps 118:99-100 (*). **a.** "Bears many things": Prov 14:17 (C). For gentle, see above at M 12. **b.** Prov 18:14 (C) (*). ὀλιγόψυχος: Prov 14:29 (contrasted with μακρόθυμος). **c, d.** Prov 26:12 (C).

M 113. **a.** Scandal: Matt 18:6; Mark 9:42; Luke 17:2; Rom 14:21; 1 Cor 8:13. ἀτιμώρητος: Prov 11:21 (C) (*); 19:5 (C), 9 (C); 28:20 (C). **b.** 1 Cor 13:5.

M 114. Num 16:30-35; Ps 105:16-18. **a.** Agitating Church: Acts 15:24; Gal 1:7; 5:10.

M 115. **a.** Ps 18:11; 80:17; 118:103; Prov 16:24; 24:13 (*); 27:7 (*). **b.** πιμπλάναι used in NT with Holy Spirit at Luke 1:15, 41, 67; Acts 2:4; 4:8, 31; 9:17; 13:9. See also Prov 15:4 (C); Sir 48:12. Compare with M 30, M 94.

M 116. **a.** τιμᾶν: Prov 3:9; 7:1 (C) (*); 14:31. **b.** δουλεύειν with Lord as object: frequent in LXX. δεικνύειν with Lord/God as subject: frequent in LXX. See also Rev 1:1.

M 117. **a.** ὑψοῦν: frequent as word for salvation in LXX, especially in Psalms. See also Prov 4:8 (*); 18:10 (*). **b.** Ps 1:3.

M 118. Matt 26:26-29; Mark 14:22-25; Luke 22:15-20; John 6:51-58; 1 Cor 10:16-21; 11:23-29.

M 119. Prov 9; Matt 26:26-29; Mark 14:22-25; Luke 22:15-20; John 6:51-58; 1 Cor 10:16-21; 11:23-29.

M 120. John 13:25; 21:20.

M 121. **a.** Prov 22:2. **b.** Matt 18:20.

M 122. **a.** "Treasure": See above references at M 25, M 87. See also Prov 2:4, 7; Wis 7:14. **b.** χάρις: Prov 12:2; 25:10 (*). χάρις καὶ ἔλεος: Wis 3:9; 4:15.

M 123. Prov 14:8 (C), 18 (*). Wisdom and prudence: Eph 1:8. **b.** ἐξιχνιάζειν: In LXX usually used for things concerning divine mysteries.

M 124. **a.** Prov 22:28 (C) (*). **b.** Prov 23:10 (C). **c.** ἐγκαταλείπειν: Jer 2:13; Ps 118:87; Prov 2:13; 4:2; 27:10 (*); 28:4. **d.** ἀπωθεῖν: Jer 6:19; Prov 1:8; 6:20; 16:3. **f.** σκεπάζειν: Ps 16:8; 26:5; 30:20; 60:4; 63:2; 90:14 (*). Evil day: Ps 90:14 (*); Prov 25:19 (*).

M 125. **a.** Job 20:15; 33:23; Prov 16:14. **b.** ἀπόλλειν: frequent in Proverbs (LXX) for losing the fruits of good works.

M 126. **a.** New beginnings with invitation to listen frequent in Proverbs as in Prov 4:10; 5:7 (C) 7:1, 24; 8:32-35; 22:17-18 (*); 23:19, 22-26. **b.** Ps 118:85 (*). ἄνομος: very common in LXX. **c.** Ps 139:4; 141:3 (*). **d.** 1 Tim 6:20 (1 Tim 2:4). **g.** Ps 13:3; 139:3. **h.** Prov 21:30. Wisdom and prudence: Eph 1:8. **i.** ἀπολλύνα: very frequent in LXX, as in Ps 5:6; frequently constructed with πάντες. **j.** πιμπλάναι with something evil: Gen 6:11, 13; Jer 28:5; Ezek 8:17; 9:9; Ps 87:3; Prov

1:31; 12:21; Sir 23:11. Compare with πιμπλάναι in
M 30, M 94, M 115 and references there. l. Acts
17:18. m. Jer 34:18. n. Col 1:28-29; Eph 6:12; 1
Tim 6:12; 2 Tim 4:7. o. Prov 13:9; John 3:19;
8:12; 2 Cor 6:14; 11:14; 1 John 1:5, 7.

M 127. a. ψευδής: very frequent in Proverbs
and throughout LXX. b. ἀπωτᾶν: Gen 3:13; Eph
5:6.

M 128. Deut 11:10-11 (C); Jer 2:18. a. Paradise of
God: Rev 2:7. b. Ps 64:9.

M 129. Deut 11:10-11 (C).

M 130. Matt 18:4; 23:12; Luke 1:48, 52; 14:11;
18:14.

M 131. Wisdom and prudence: Eph 1:8. a.
ὑψοῦν: frequent as word for salvation in LXX,
especially in Psalms; see also Prov 4:8 (*);
18:10 (*). b. Pure heart: Matt 5:8; 1 Tim 1:5; 2
Tim 2:22.

M 132. Prov 20:5; Rom 11:33. a. σκοτεινός: Ps
72:16 (*); 118:7 (*); Matt 6:23; Luke 11:34-36.

M 133. a. Purity with seeing: Ps 23:3-4; Matt
5:8. b. For gentle, see above at M 12.

M 134. b. ἀθετεῖν: Luke 10:16; John 12:48.

M 135. a. πλατύνειν with heart: Ps 4:2 (*);
17:36 (*); 118:32 (*), 96 (*); Prov 1:20-21 (*); 18:16
(*); 22:20 (*); 2 Cor 6:11, 13. b. ὑψοῦν: frequent

as word for salvation in LXX, especially in Psalms; see also Prov 4:8 (*); 18:10 (*).

M 136. b. *παριστάναι:* Rom 6:13; 2 Cor 4:14; 11:2; Col 1:21-22, 28; 2 Tim 2:15.

Guide to Further Reading

Most of the writing on Evagrius can be rather difficult, and so it is not easy to suggest further reading that would not be of a technical nature. I have written a longer study on *Ad Monachos* which may interest the reader who wants to pursue Evagrius further and in which a long bibliography may be found. See J. Driscoll, *The* 'Ad Monachos' *of Evagrius Ponticus, Its Structure and a Select Commentary* (Rome: Studia Anselmiana, 1991.) Other studies in English which may be helpful either on Evagrius or on the general background of the Egyptian Desert Monasticism of the fourth century would include the following:

Bamberger, J. E. *Evagrius Ponticus. The Praktikos. Chapters on Prayer.* Cistercian Studies, no. 4. Kalamazoo, 1981.

Bunge, G. "The 'Spiritual Prayer': On the Trinitarian Mysticism of Evagrius of Pontus." *Monastic Studies* 17 (1987) 191–208.

Burton-Christie, D. *The Word in the Desert: Scripture and the Quest for Holiness in Early Christian Monasticism.* Oxford, 1992.

Chitty, D. J. *The Desert a City,* Oxford, 1966.

Dechow, J. F. *Dogma and Mysticism in Early Christianity: Epiphanius of Cyprus and the Legacy of Origen.* Macon, Ga., 1988.

Driscoll, J. "Listlessness in *The Mirror for Monks* of Evagrius Ponticus." *Cistercian Studies* 24 (1989) 206–214.

———. "Gentleness in the *Ad Monachos* of Evagrius Ponticus." *Studia Monastica* 32 (1990): 295–321.

Elm, S. "The *Sententiae ad Virginem* by Evagrius Ponticus and the Problem of Early Monastic Rules." *Augustinianum* 30 (1990) 393-404.

Kline, F. "The Christology of Evagrius and the Parent System of Origen." *Cistercian Studies* (1985) 155-183.

Louth, A. *The Origins of the Christian Mystical Tradition. From Plato to Denys.* Oxford, 1981.

O'Laughlin, M. "Evagrius Ponticus, *Antirrheticus* (Selections)" in V. Wimbush, ed., *Ascetic Behavior in Greco-Roman Antiquity, A Sourcebook.* Minneapolis, 1990.

———. "The Bible, the Deomons, and the Desert: Evaluating the *Antirrheticus* of Evagrius Ponticus" in *Studia Monastica* 34 (1992) 201-215.

Parmentier, M. "Evagrius of Pontus and the 'Letter to Melania.'" *Bijdragen, tijdschrift voor filosofie en theologie* 46 (1985) 2-38.

Tugwell, S. *Ways of Imperfection: an Exploration of Christian Spirituality.* Springfield, Ill., 1985.